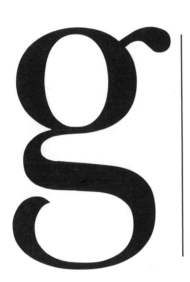

GEOMETRY

GRE Math Strategy Guide

This volume guides students through the intricacies of shapes, planes, lines, angles, and objects, illustrating every geometric principle, formula, and problem type tested on the GRE.

Geometry GRE Strategy Guide, First Edition

10-digit International Standard Book Number: 1-935707-04-3
13-digit International Standard Book Number: 978-1-935707-04-2

8 GUIDE INSTRUCTIONAL SERIES

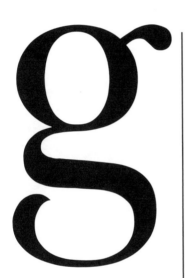

Math GRE Strategy Guides

Algebra
(ISBN: 978-1-935707-02-8)

Fractions, Decimals, & Percents
(ISBN: 978-1-935707-03-5)

Geometry
(ISBN: 978-1-935707-04-2)

Number Properties
(ISBN: 978-1-935707-05-9)

Word Translations
(ISBN: 978-1-935707-06-6)

Quantitative Comparisons & Data Interpretation
(ISBN: 978-1-935707-07-3)

Verbal GRE Strategy Guides

Reading Comprehension & Essays
(ISBN: 978-1-935707-08-0)

ASA: Antonyms, Sentence Completion, Analogies
(ISBN: 978-1-935707-09-7)

*Manhattan*GRE

September 1st, 2010

Dear Student,

Thank you for picking up one of the Manhattan GRE Strategy Guides—we hope that it refreshes your memory of junior-high school math that you haven't used in years. Maybe it will even teach you a new thing or two.

As with most accomplishments, there were many people involved in the book that you're holding. First and foremost is Zeke Vanderhoek, the founder of MG Prep. Zeke was a lone tutor in New York when he started the Company in 2000. Now, ten years later, the Company has Instructors and offices nationwide and contributes to the studies and successes of thousands of students each year.

Our Manhattan GRE Strategy Guides are based on the continuing experiences of our Instructors and our students. On the Company side, we are indebted to many of our Instructors, including but not limited to Jen Dziura, Stacey Koprince, David Mahler, Chris Ryan, Michael Schwartz, and Tommy Wallach, all of whom either wrote or edited the books to their present form. Dan McNaney and Cathy Huang provided their formatting expertise to make the books as user-friendly as possible. Last, many people, too numerous to list here but no less appreciated, assisted in the development of the online resources that accompany this guide.

At Manhattan GRE, we continually aspire to provide the best Instructors and resources possible. We hope that you'll find our dedication manifest in this book. If you have any comments or questions, please e-mail me at andrew.yang@manhattangre.com. I'll be sure that your comments reach Chris and the rest of the team—and I'll read them too.

Best of luck in preparing for the GRE!

Sincerely,

Andrew Yang
President
Manhattan GRE

HOW TO ACCESS YOUR ONLINE STUDY CENTER

If you...

⊙ ## are a registered Manhattan GRE student

and have received this book as part of your course materials, you have AUTOMATIC access to ALL of our online resources. To access these resources, follow the instructions in the Welcome Guide provided to you at the start of your program. Do NOT follow the instructions below.

⊙ ## purchased this book from the Manhattan GRE Online store or at one of our Centers

1. Go to: http://www.manhattangre.com/studycenter.cfm

2. Log in using the username and password used when your account was set up.

⊙ ## purchased this book at a retail location

1. Go to: http://www.manhattangre.com/access.cfm

2. Log in or create an account.

3. Follow the instructions on the screen.

Your one year of online access begins on the day that you register your book at the above URL.

You only need to register your product ONCE at the above URL. To use your online resources any time AFTER you have completed the registration process, login to the following URL: http://www.manhattangre.com/studycenter.cfm

Please note that online access is non-transferable. This means that only NEW and UNREGISTERED copies of the book will grant you online access. Previously used books will not provide any online resources.

⊙ ## purchased an e-book version of this book

Email a copy of your purchase receipt to books@manhattangre.com to activate your resources.

For any technical issues, email books@manhattangre.com or call 800-576-4628.

Introduction, and How to Use Manhattan GRE's Strategy Guides

We know that you're looking to succeed on the GRE so that you can go to graduate school and do the things you want to do in life.

We also know that you might not have done math since high school, and that you may never have learned words like "adumbrate" or "sangfroid." We know that it's going to take hard work on your part to get a top GRE score, and that's why we've put together the only set of books that will take you from the basics all the way up to the material you need to master for a near-perfect score, or whatever your score goal may be.

How a Computer Adaptive Test Works

On paper-based tests, top scores are achieved by solving a mix of easy and medium questions, with a few hard ones at the end. The GRE is totally different.

The GRE is a computer adaptive test (or "CAT"). That means that the better you do, the harder the material you will see (and the worse you do, the easier the material you will see). Your ultimate score isn't based on how many questions you got right—it's based on "testing into" a high level of difficulty, and then performing well enough to stay at that difficulty level. In other words, you *want* to see mostly hard questions.

This book was written by a team of test prep professionals, including instructors who have scored perfect 1600s repeatedly on the GRE, and who have taught and tutored literally thousands of students at all levels of performance. We don't just focus on "tricks"—on a test that adapts to your performance, it's important to know the real material being tested.

Speed and Pacing

Most people can sum up the numbers from 1–20, if they have enough time. Most people can also tell you whether 789×791 is bigger than 788×792, if they have enough time. Few people can do these things in the 1–2 minutes per problem allotted on the GRE.

If you've taken a practice test (visit www.manhattangre.com for information about this), you may have had serious trouble finishing the test before time ran out. On the GRE, it is extremely important that you finish every question. (You also may not skip questions or return to any previously answered question). In these books, you'll find ways to do things fast—very fast.

As a reference, here's about how much time you should spend on each problem type on the GRE:

Analogies – **45 seconds**

Sentence Correction – **1 minute**

Problem Solving and Data Interpretation – **2 minutes**

Antonyms – **30 seconds**

Reading Comprehension – **1.5 minutes**

Quantitative Comparison – **1 min 15 seconds**

Of course, no one can time each question this precisely while taking the actual test—instead, you will see a timer on the screen that counts down (from 30 minutes on Verbal, and from 45 minutes on Quant), and you must keep an eye on that clock and manage time as you go. Manhattan GRE's strategies will help you solve questions extremely efficiently.

How to Use These Materials

Manhattan GRE's materials are comprehensive. But keep in mind that, depending on your score goal, it may not be necessary to "get" absolutely everything. Grad schools only see your overall Quantitative, Verbal, and Writing scores—they don't see exactly which strengths and weaknesses went into creating those scores.

You may be enrolled in one of our courses, in which case you already have a syllabus telling you in what order you should approach the books. But if you bought this book online or at a bookstore, feel free to approach the books—and even the chapters within the books—in whatever order works best for you. *For the most part, the books, and the chapters within them, are independent; you don't have to master one section before moving on to the next.* So if you're having a hard time with something in particular, you can make a note to come back to it later and move on to another section. Similarly, it may not be necessary to solve every single practice problem for every section. As you go through the material, continually assess whether you understand and can apply the principles in each individual section and chapter. The best way to do this is to solve the Check Your Skills and Practice Problems throughout. If you're confident you have a concept or method down, feel free to move on. If you struggle with something, make note of it for further review. Stay active in your learning and oriented toward the test—it's easy to read something and think you understand it, only to have trouble applying it in the 1–2 minutes you have to solve a problem.

Study Skills

As you're studying for the GRE, try to integrate your learning into your everyday life. For example, vocabulary is a big part of the GRE, as well as something you just can't "cram" for—you're going to want to do at least a little bit of vocab every day. So, try to learn and internalize a little bit at a time, switching up topics often to help keep things interesting.

Keep in mind that, while many of your study materials are on paper (including ETS's most recent source of official GRE questions, *Practicing to Take the GRE General Test 10th Edition*), your exam will be administered on a computer. The testing center will provide you with pencils and a booklet of bound, light-blue paper. If you run out, you may request a new booklet, but you may only have one at a time. Because this is a computer-based test, you will NOT be able to underline portions of reading passages, write on diagrams of geometry figures, or otherwise physically mark up problems. So get used to this now. Solve the problems in these books on scratch paper. (Each of our books talks specifically about what to write down for different problem types).

Again, as you study stay focused on the test-day experience. As you progress, work on timed drills and sets of questions. Eventually, you should be taking full practice tests (available at www.manhattangre.com) under realistic timed conditions.

Changes to the Exam

Finally, you've probably heard that the GRE is changing in August, 2011. Look in the back of this book for more information about the switch—every one of these GRE books contains additional material for the 2011 GRE, and we'll be constantly updating www.manhattangre.com as new information becomes available. If you're going to take the test before the changeover, it's nothing to worry about.

Diving In

While we love standardized tests, we understand that your goal is really about grad school, and your life beyond that. However, you'll make your way through these books much more easily—and much more pleasantly—if you can stay positive and engaged throughout. Hopefully, the process of studying for the GRE will make your brain a more interesting place to be! Now let's get started!

TABLE OF CONTENTS

g

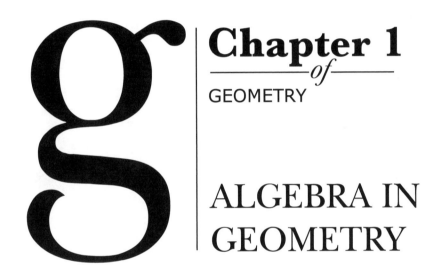

Chapter 1
of
GEOMETRY

ALGEBRA IN GEOMETRY

In This Chapter . . .

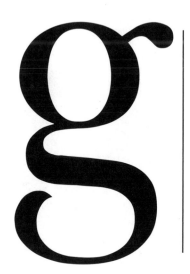

- Using Equations to Solve Geometry Problems

Using Equations to Solve Geometry Problems

Before we dive into the specific properties of the many shapes tested on the GRE, it's important to establish a foundation of translating the information presented in questions into algebraic equations. This will allow us to more easily, and quickly, solve even the most complex geometry problems. To start, let's do the following problem together.

Rectangles *ABCD* and *EFGH*, shown below, have equal areas. The length of side *AB* is 5. What is the length of diagonal *AC*?

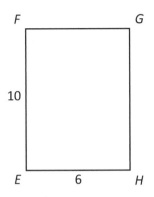
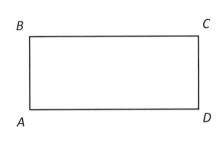

The first step in any geometry question involving shapes is to draw your own copies of the shapes on your note paper and fill in everything you know. In this problem in particular, you would want to redraw both rectangles and add to your picture the information that side *AB* has a length of 5. Also, make note of what you're looking for—in this case we want the length of diagonal *AC*. So your new figures would look like this:

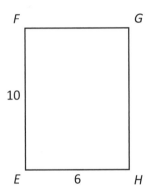
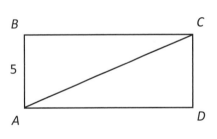

Now that we have redrawn our figures and filled in all the given information, it's time to begin answering the question. Realize that many geometry questions are similar to the word problems discussed in the Word Translations Strategy Guide. Both types of problems provide us with information that describes relationships that can be expressed mathematically. The only difference is that sometimes this information is stated in words, and sometimes it's presented visually.

So now the question becomes—has the question provided us any information that can be expressed mathematically? In other words, can we create equations? Well, they did tell us one thing that we can use—the two rectangles have equal areas. So we can say that Area$_{ABCD}$ = Area$_{EFGH}$. But we can do better than that. The formula for area of a rectangle is Area = (length) × (width). So our equation can be rewritten as (length$_{ABCD}$) × (width$_{ABCD}$) = (length$_{EFGH}$) × (width$_{EFGH}$).

The length and width of rectangle *EFGH* are 6 and 10 (it doesn't matter which is which) and the length of *AB* is 5. So our equation becomes $(5) \times (\text{width}_{ABCD}) = (6) \times (10)$. So $(5) \times (\text{width}_{ABCD}) = 60$, which means that the width of rectangle *ABCD* equals 12.

Any time you learn a new piece of information (in this case the width of rectangle *ABCD*) you should put that information into your picture. So our picture of rectangle *ABCD* now looks like this:

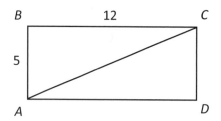

To recap what we've done so far, we started this problem by redrawing the shapes described in the question and filling in all the information (such as side lengths, angles, etc.) that we knew, and made note of the value the question was asking us for. Just as the first steps for solving word problems are to identify unknowns, create variables, and write down givens, the first step for geometry problems is to **draw or redraw figures and fill in all given information.** Of course, we should also confirm what we're being asked!

Next we made use of additional information provided in the question. The question stated that the two rectangles had equal areas. We created an equation to express this relationship, and then plugged in the values we knew (length and width of rectangle *EFGH* and length of rectangle *ABCD*) and solved for the width of rectangle *ABCD*. This process was identical to the process used to solve word problems—we **identified relationships and created equations.** After that, we **solved the equations for the missing value** (in this case, the width of *ABCD*).

In some ways, all we have done so far is set up the problem. In fact, aside from noting that we need to find the length of diagonal *AC*, nothing we have done so far seems to have directly helped us actually solve for that value. The result of the work we've done to this point is to find that the width of rectangle *ABCD* is 12.

So why did we bother solving for the width of rectangle *ABCD* when we didn't even know why we would need it? The answer is that there is a very good chance that we will need that value in order to answer the question.

There was no way initially to find the length of diagonal *AC*. We simply did not have enough information. The question did, however, provide us enough information to find the width of rectangle *ABCD*. More often than not, if you have enough information to solve for a value, you need that value to answer the question.

So the question now becomes, what can we do now that we know the width of *ABCD* that we couldn't do before? To answer that, let's take another look at the value we're looking for: the length of *AC*.

As mentioned earlier, an important part of problem solving is to identify relationships. We already identified the relationship mentioned in the question—that both rectangles have equal areas. But for many geometry problems there are additional relationships that aren't as obvious.

The key to this problem is to recognize that *AC* is not only the diagonal of rectangle *ABCD*, but is also the hypotenuse of a right triangle. We know this because one property of rectangles is that all four interior angles are right angles.

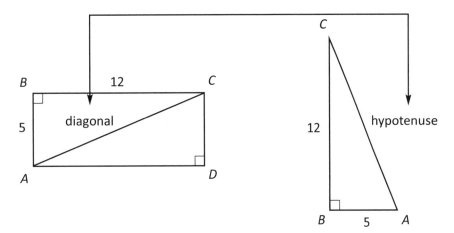

Now that we know *AC* is the hypotenuse of a right triangle, we can use the Pythagorean Theorem to find the length of the hypotenuse using the two side lengths.

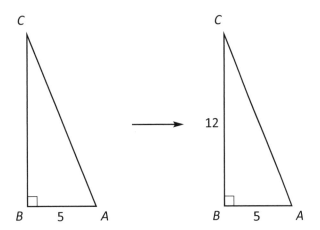

Sides *BC* and *AB* are the legs of the triangle, and *AC* is the hypotenuse, so:

$$(BC)^2 + (AB)^2 = (AC)^2$$
$$(12)^2 + (5)^2 = (AC)^2$$
$$144 + 25 = (AC)^2$$
$$169 = (AC)^2$$
$$13 = AC$$

Alternatively, you can avoid that work by recognizing that this triangle is one of the Pythagorean triplets: a 5–12–13 triangle. Either way, the answer to the question is *AC* = 13.

Let's recap what we did in the last portion of this question. The process that allowed us to solve for the width of *ABCD* was based on information explicitly presented to us in the question. To proceed from there, however, required a different sort of process. The key insight was that the diagonal of rectangle *ABCD* was also the hypotenuse of right triangle *ABC*. Additionally, we needed to know that, in order to find the length of *AC*, we needed the lengths of the other two sides of the triangle. The last part of this problem required us to **make inferences from the figures.** Sometimes these inferences require you to make a jump from one shape to another through a common element. For instance, we needed to see *AC* as both a diagonal of a rectangle and as a hypotenuse of a right triangle. Here *AC* was the common element in both a rectangle and a right triangle. Other times, these inferences make you think about what information you would need in order to find another value.

In a moment, we'll go through another sample problem, but before we do, let's revisit the important steps to answering geometry problems.

Recap:

Step 1: **Draw or redraw figures and fill in all given information.**
   Fill in all known angles and lengths and make note of any equal sides or angles.

Step 2: **Identify relationships and create equations.**
   Often these relationships will be explicitly stated in the question.

Step 3: **Solve the equations for the missing value.**
   If you can solve for a value, you will often need that value to answer the question.

Step 4: **Make inferences from the figures.**
   You will often need to make use of relationships that are not explicitly stated.

Now that we've got the basic process down, let's do another problem. Try it on your own first, then we'll walk through it together.

Rectangle *PQRS* is inscribed in Circle *O* pictured below. The center of Circle *O* is also the center of Rectangle *PQRS*. If the circumference of Circle *O* is 5π, what is the area of Rectangle *PQRS*?

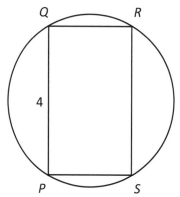

The first thing you should have done is **redraw the figure** on whatever note paper you are using and **fill in all the given information.** The question didn't explicitly give us the value of any side lengths or angles, but it did say that *PQRS* is a rectangle. That means all 4 internal angles are right angles. So when you redraw the figure, it might look like this.

Manhattan **GRE** Prep
the new standard

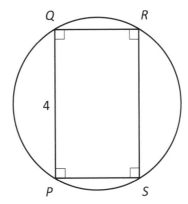

Now it's time to **identify relationships and create equations.** The question stated that the circumference of Circle O is 5π, and we know the formula for circumference. Circumference equals $2\pi r$, so $5\pi = 2\pi r$. Now that we know the circumference, there's only one unknown (r), so we should **solve the equation for the missing value** and find the radius, which turns out to be 2.5. We also know that $d = 2r$, so the diameter of Circle O is 5.

As with the previous problem, we are now left with the question—why did we find the radius and diameter? We were able to solve for them, which is a very good clue that we need one of them to answer the question. Now is the time to **make inferences from the figures.**

Ultimately, this question is asking for the area of rectangle $PQRS$. What information do we need to find that value? We have the length of QP, which means that if we can find the length of either QR or PS, we can find the area of the rectangle. So we need to somehow find a connection between the rectangle and the radius or diameter. Let's put a diameter into the circle.

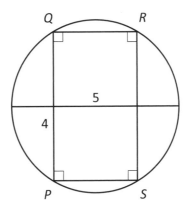

That didn't really seem to help much, because we still have no way to make the connection between the diameter and the rectangle. It's important to remember, though, that *any* line that passes through the center is a diameter. What if we drew the diameter so that it passed through the center but touched the circle at points P and R? We know that the line connecting points P and R will be a diameter because we know that the center of the circle is also the center of the rectangle. Our circle now looks like this:

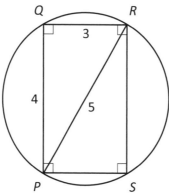

What was the advantage of drawing the diameter so that it connected points *P* and *R*? Now the diameter of the circle is also the diagonal of the rectangle. The circle and the rectangle have a common element.

Where do we go from here? We still need the length of either *QR* or *PS*. Do we have a way to get either one of those values? As a matter of fact, we do. *PQR* is a right triangle. It's not oriented the way we are used to seeing it, but all the important elements are there. It's a triangle, and one of its internal angles is a right angle. Additionally, we know the lengths of 2 of the sides: *QP* and *PR*. That means we can use the Pythagorean Theorem to find the length of the third side: *QR*.

$$(QR)^2 + (QP)^2 = (PR)^2$$
$$(QR)^2 + (4)^2 = (5)^2$$
$$(QR)^2 + 16 = 25$$
$$(QR)^2 = 9$$
$$QR = 3$$

Alternatively, we could have recognized the Pythagorean triplet—triangle *PQR* is a 3–4–5 triangle. Either way we arrive at the conclusion that the length of *QR* is 3. Our circle now looks like this:

Now we have what we need to find the area of rectangle *PQRS*. Area = (length) × (width) = (4) × (3) = 12. So the answer to the question is 12.

What did we need to do in order to arrive at that answer? For starters, we needed to make sure that we had an accurate figure to work with, and that we populated that figure with all the information that had been given to us. Next we had to realize that knowing the circumference of the circle allowed us to find the diameter of the circle.

After that came what is often the most difficult part of the process—we had to make inferences based on the figure. The key insight in this problem was that we could draw a diameter in our figure that could also act as the diagonal of the rectangle. As if that wasn't difficult enough, we then had to recognize that *PQR* was a right triangle, even though it was rotated in a way that made it difficult to see. It is these kinds of insights that are going to be crucial to success on the GRE—recognizing shapes when they're presented in an unfamiliar format and finding connections between different shapes.

Check Your Skills

1. In rectangle *ABCD*, the distance from *A* to *C* is 10. What is the area of the circle inside the rectangle, if this circle touches both *AD* and *BC*? (This is known as an inscribed circle).

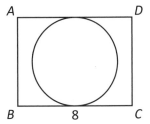

The answer can be found on page 21.

Check Your Skills Answers

1. **9π:** Redraw the diagram *without* the circle, so you can focus on the rectangle. Add in the diagonal *AC*, since we're given its length.

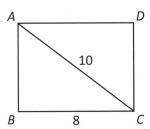

Now we look at right triangle *ABC*. *AC* functions not only as the diagonal of rectangle *ABCD* but also as the hypotenuse of right triangle *ABC*. So now we find the third side of triangle *ABC*, either using the Pythagorean Theorem or recognizing a Pythagorean triplet (6–8–10).

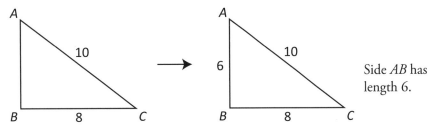

Side *AB* has length 6.

$(AB)^2 + 8^2 = 10^2$
$(AB)^2 + 64 = 100$
$(AB)^2 = 36$
$AB = 6$

Now, we redraw the diagram *with* the circle but without the diagonal, since we've gotten what we needed from that: the other side of the rectangle.

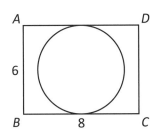

Since the circle touches both *AD* and *BC*, we know that its diameter must be 6.

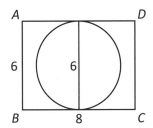

Finally, we find the radius and compute the area:

$d = 6 = 2r$ Area $= \pi r^2$
$3 = r$ $= \pi 3^2$
                        Area $= 9\pi$

Problem Set

1.

The "aspect ratio" of a rectangular TV screen is the ratio of its height to its width.

Column A

The area of a rectangular TV screen with an aspect ratio of 3:4 and a diagonal of 25"

Column B

The area of a rectangular TV screen with an aspect ratio of 9:16 and a diagonal of 25"

2.

Ten 8-foot long poles will be arranged in a rectangle to surround a flowerbed.

Column A

The area in square feet of the flowerbed

Column B

300

3.

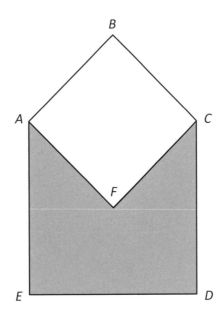

ABCF and *ACDE* are squares.

Column A

Twice the area of the shaded region

Column B

Three times the area of *ABCF*

1. **A:** For any fixed diagonal, as for any fixed perimeter, the rectangle with the greatest area is a square. Given two rectangles with equal diagonals, the one that is more nearly square has a greater area. A 3 : 4 ratio is more nearly square (closer to 1) than is a 9 : 16 ratio.

Each of the following rectangles has the same diagonal. Compare their areas.

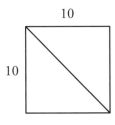
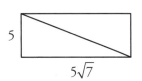

The area of the square is larger, and is the largest possible area for the diagonal of that length. As the diagonal rotates, the area of the rectangle gets progressively smaller.

2. **D:** There are two possible ways to arrange the poles into rectangles, 2 poles × 3 poles, and 1 pole × 4 poles. The 2 × 3 arrangement will enclose an area 16 × 24, which is more than 300 square feet. The 1 × 4 arrangement will enclose an area 8 × 32, which is less than 300 square feet.

Ten 8-foot long poles will be arranged in a rectangle to surround a flowerbed.

Column A

The area in square feet of the flowerbed =

16 × 24 = **384** OR
8 × 32 = **256**

Column B

300

3. **C:** The simplest solution is to draw the diagonals of the larger square and add the line *AC*. This yields a combined figure cut into five equal triangles:

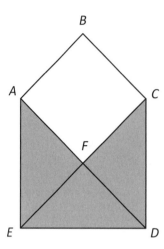

The shaded region is three such triangles, so Column A represents the area of six such triangles. *ABCF* is two such triangles, so Column B represents the area of six such triangles.

There are also algebraic solutions to this problem, although they're all reasonably complicated. Here's one: Since the ratio of the diagonal of a square to its side is $\sqrt{2} : 1$, $AC = \sqrt{2}\,AB$.

So the area of the large square is $(\sqrt{2}AB)^2$, or $2(AB)^2$.
The area of the smaller square is simply $(AB)^2$.

The shaded region represents 3/4 the area $2(AB)^2$, or $\dfrac{3}{2}(AB)^2$.

We can rewrite the columns.

Column A

Twice the area of the shaded region

$$= 2 \cdot \frac{3}{2}(AB)^2 = \mathbf{3(AB)^2}$$

Column B

Three times the area of
$ABCF = 3 \cdot (AB)^2 = \mathbf{3(AB)^2}$

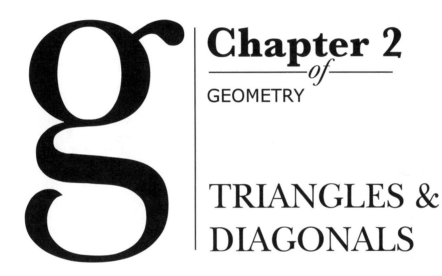

Chapter 2

of

GEOMETRY

TRIANGLES &
DIAGONALS

In This Chapter . . .

- The Basic Properties of a Triangle
- Perimeter and Area
- Right Triangles
- Pythagorean Triplets
- Isosceles Triangles and the 45–45–90 Triangle
- Equilateral Triangles and the 30–60–90 Triangle
- Diagonals of Other Polygons

The Basic Properties of a Triangle

Triangles show up all over the GRE. You'll often find them hiding in problems that seem to be about rectangles or other shapes. Of the basic shapes, triangles are perhaps the most challenging to master. One reason is that several properties of triangles are tested.

Let's start with some general comments on triangles:

The sum of any two side lengths of a triangle will always be greater than the third side length. This is because the shortest distance between two points is a straight line. At the same time, the third side length will always be greater than the difference of the other two side lengths. The pictures below illustrate these two points.

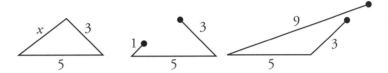

What is the largest number x could be? What's the smallest? Could it be 9? 1?

> x must be less than $3 + 5 = 8$
> x must be greater than $5 - 3 = 2$
> $2 < x < 8$

Check Your Skills

1. Two sides of a triangle have lengths 5 and 19. Can the third side have a length of 13?
2. Two sides of a triangle have lengths 8 and 17. What is the range of possible values of the length of the third side?

Answers can be found on page 41.

The internal angles of a triangle must add up to 180°. This rule can sometimes allow us to make inferences about angles of unknown size. It means that if we know the measures of 2 angles in the triangle, we can determine the measure of the third angle. Take a look at this triangle:

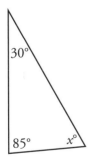

The 3 internal angles must add up to 180°, so we know that $30 + 85 + x = 180$. Solving for x tells us that $x = 65$. So the third angle is 65°. The GRE can also test your knowledge of this rule in more complicated ways. Take a look at this triangle:

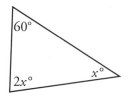

In this situation, we only know one of the angles. The other 2 are given in terms of x. Even though we only know one angle, we can still determine the other 2. Again, we know that the 3 angles will add up to 180. So $60 + x + 2x = 180$. That means that $3x = 120$. So $x = 40$. Thus the angle labeled $x°$ has a measure of 40° and the angle labeled $2x°$ has a measure of 80°.

The GRE will not always draw triangles to scale, so don't try to guess angles from the picture, which could be distorted. Instead, solve for angles mathematically.

Check Your Skills

Find the missing angle(s).

3.

4.

5.

Answers can be found on pages 41.

Internal angles of a triangle are important on the GRE for another reason. Sides correspond to their opposite angles. This means that the longest side is opposite the largest angle, and the smallest side is opposite the smallest angle. Think about an alligator opening its mouth, bigger and bigger… as the angle between its upper and lower jaws increases, the distance between the front teeth on the bottom and top jaws would get longer and longer.

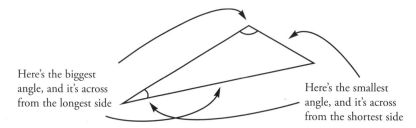

Here's the biggest angle, and it's across from the longest side

Here's the smallest angle, and it's across from the shortest side

One important thing to remember about this relationship is that it works both ways. If we know the sides of the triangle, we can make inferences about the angles. If we know the angles, we can make inferences about the sides.

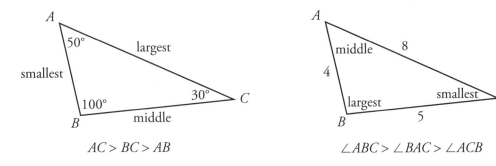

$$AC > BC > AB$$ $$\angle ABC > \angle BAC > \angle ACB$$

Although we can determine from the angle measures which sides are longer, which sides are shorter, and which sides are equal, we cannot determine how MUCH greater or shorter. For instance, in the triangle above, $\angle ABC$ is twice as large as $\angle BAC$, but that does not mean that AC is twice as large as BC.

Things get interesting when a triangle has sides that are the same length or angles that have the same measure. We can classify triangles by the number of equal sides that they have.

- A triangle that has 2 equal angles and 2 equal sides (opposite the equal angles) is an **isosceles triangle.**

- A triangle that has 3 equal angles (all 60°) and 3 equal sides is an **equilateral triangle.**

Once again, it is important to remember that this relationship between equal angles and equal sides works in both directions. Take a look at these isosceles triangles, and think about what additional information we can infer from them.

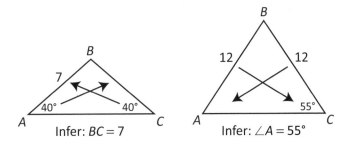

The GRE loves isosceles triangles and uses them in a variety of ways. The following is a more challenging application of the equal sides/equal angles rule.

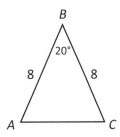

Take a look at the triangle and see what other information you can fill in. Specifically, do you know the degree measure of either *BAC* or *BCA*?

Because side *AB* is the same length as side *BC*, we know that *BAC* has the same degree measure as *BCA*. For convenience we could label each of those angles as $x°$ on our diagram.

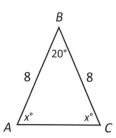

We also know that the 3 internal angles will add up to 180. So $20 + x + x = 180$. $2x = 160$, and $x = 80$. So *BAC* and *BCA* each equal 80°. We can't find the side length *AC* without more advanced math, but the GRE wouldn't ask you for this side length for that very reason.

Check Your Skills
Find the value of *x*.

6.

7.

8.

Answers can be found on pages 41–42.

Perimeter and Area

The **perimeter** of a triangle is the sum of the lengths of all 3 sides.

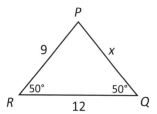

In this triangle, the perimeter is $5 + 6 + 10 = 21$. This is a relatively simple property of a triangle, so often it will be used in combination with another property. Try this next problem. What is the perimeter of triangle *PQR*?

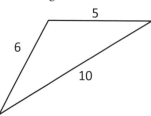

To solve for the perimeter, we will need to determine the value of *x*. Because angles *PQR* and *PRQ* are both 50°, we know that their opposite sides will have equal lengths. That means sides *PR* and *PQ* must have equal lengths, so we can infer that side *PQ* has a length of 9. The perimeter of triangle *PQR* is 9 + 9 + 12 = 30.

Check Your Skills

What is the perimeter of each triangle?

9.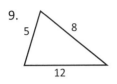

10.

Answers can be found on page 42.

Note: Figures not drawn to scale. You need to be ready to solve geometry problems without depending on exactly accurate figures.

The final property of a triangle we will discuss is area. You may be familiar with the equation Area = 1/2 (base) × (height). One very important thing to understand about the area of a triangle (and area in general) is the relationship between the base and the height. The base and the height MUST be perpendicular to each other. In a triangle, one side of the triangle is the base, and the height is formed by dropping a line from the third point of the triangle straight down towards the base, so that it forms a 90° angle with the base. The small square located where the height and base meet (in the figure below) is a very common symbol used to denote a right angle.

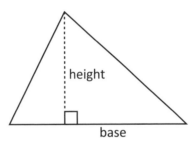

An additional challenge on the GRE is that problems will ask you about familiar shapes but present them to you in orientations you are unused to. Even the area of a triangle is affected. Most people generally think of the base of the triangle as the bottom side of the triangle, but in reality, any side of the triangle could act as a base. In fact, depending on the orientation of the triangle, there may not actually be a bottom side. The three triangles below are all the same triangle, but in each one we have made a different side the base, and drawn in the corresponding height.

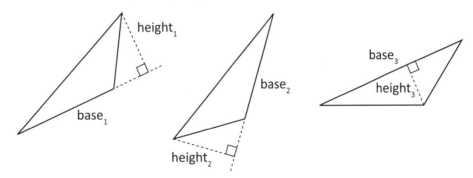

As it turns out, not only can any side be the base, but the height doesn't even need to appear in the triangle! The only thing that matters is that the base and the height are perpendicular to each other.

Check Your Skills

What are the areas of the following triangles?

11.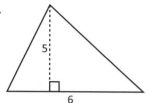

12.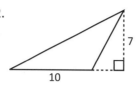

Answers can be found on page 42–43.

Right Triangles

There is one more class of triangle that is very common on the GRE: the **right triangle.** A right triangle is any triangle in which one of the angles is a right angle. The reason they are so important will become more clear as we attempt to answer the next question.

What is the perimeter of triangle *ABC*?

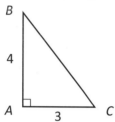

Normally we would be unable to answer this question. We only have two sides of the triangle, but we need all three sides to calculate the perimeter.

The reason we can answer this question is that right triangles have an additional property that the GRE likes to make use of: there is a consistent relationship among the lengths of its sides. This relationship is known as the **Pythagorean Theorem.** For *any* right triangle, the relationship is $a^2 + b^2 = c^2$, where a and b are the lengths of the sides touching the right angle, also known as **legs**, and c is the length of the side opposite the right angle, also known as the **hypotenuse.**

In the above triangle, sides *AB* and *AC* are a and b (it doesn't matter which is which) and side *BC* is c. So $(3)^2 + (4)^2 = (BC)^2$. $9 + 16 = (BC)^2$, so $25 = (BC)^2$, and the length of side *BC* is 5. Our triangle really looks like this:

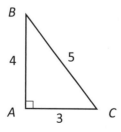

Finally, the perimeter = 3 + 4 + 5 = 12.

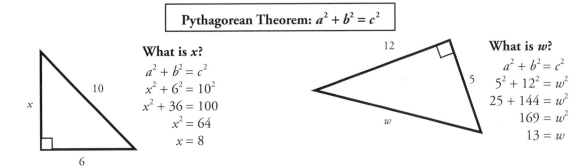

Pythagorean Triplets

As mentioned above, right triangles show up in many problems on the GRE, and many of these problems require the Pythagorean Theorem. But there is a shortcut that we can use in many situations to make the calculations easier.

The GRE favors a certain subset of right triangles in which all three sides have lengths that are integer values. The triangle we saw above was an example of that. The lengths of the sides were 3, 4 and 5—all integers. This group of side lengths is a **Pythagorean triplet**—a 3–4–5 triangle. Although there is an infinite number of Pythagorean triplets, a few are likely to appear on the test and should be memorized. For each triplet, the first two numbers are the lengths of the sides that *touch the right angle*, and the third (and largest) number is the *length of the hypotenuse*. They are:

Common Combinations	**Key Multiples**
3–4–5	6–8–10
The most popular of all right triangles	9–12–15
$3^2 + 4^2 = 5^2$ (9 + 16 = 25)	12–16–20
5–12–13	
Also quite popular on the GRE	10–24–26
$5^2 + 12^2 = 13^2$ (25 + 144 = 169)	
8–15–17	
This one appears less frequently	None
$8^2 + 15^2 = 17^2$ (64 + 225 = 289)	

Warning! Even as you memorize these triangles, don't assume that all triangles fall into these categories. When using common combinations to solve a problem, be sure that the triangle is a right triangle, and that the largest side (hypotenuse) corresponds to the largest number in the triplet. For example, if you have a right triangle with one side measuring 3 and the hypotenuse measuring 4, DO NOT conclude that the remaining side is 5.

That being said, let's look at a practice question to see how memorizing these triplets can save us time on the GRE.

What is the area of triangle *DEF*?

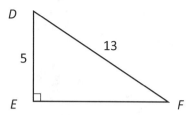

What do we need in order to find the area of triangle *DEF*? Like any triangle, the formula is area = 1/2 (base) × (height), so we need a base and a height. This is a right triangle, so sides *DE* and *EF* are perpendicular to each other, which means that if we can figure out the length of side *EF*, we can calculate the area.

The question then becomes, how do we find the length of side *EF*? First, realize that we can *always* find the length of the third side of a right triangle if we know the lengths of the other two sides. That's because we know the Pythagorean Theorem. In this case, the formula would look like this: $(DE)^2 + (EF)^2 = (DF)^2$. We know the lengths of two of those sides, so we could rewrite the equation as $(5)^2 + (EF)^2 = (13)^2$. Solving this equation, we get $25 + (EF)^2 = 169$, so $(EF)^2 = 144$, which means $EF = 12$. But these calculations are unnecessary; once you see a right triangle in which one of the legs has a length of 5 and the hypotenuse has a length of 13, you should recognize the Pythagorean triplet. The length of the other leg must be 12.

However you find the length of side *EF*, our triangle now looks like this:

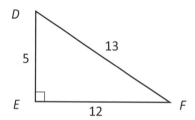

Now we have what we need to find the area of triangle *DEF*. Area = $^1/_2(12) \times (5) = ^1/_2(60) = 30$. Note that in a right triangle, you can consider one leg the base and the other leg the height.

Check Your Skills
For #13–15, what is the length of the third side of the triangle? For #15, find the area.

13.   14. 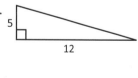   15.

16. What is the value of hypotenuse *C*? (pictured right)

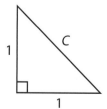

17. What is the value of leg *B*? (pictured right)

18. Triangle *ABC* is isosceles. If *AB* = 3, and *BC* = 4, what are the possible lengths of *AC*?

Answers can be found on page 43.

Isosceles Triangles and the 45–45–90 Triangle

As previously noted, an isosceles triangle is one in which two sides are equal. The two angles opposite those two sides will also be equal. The most important isosceles triangle on the GRE is the isosceles right triangle.

An isosceles right triangle has one 90° angle (opposite the hypotenuse) and two 45° angles (opposite the two equal legs). This triangle is called the 45–45–90 triangle.

The lengths of the legs of every 45–45–90 triangle have a specific ratio, which you must memorize:

45° → 45° → 90°		
leg	leg	hypotenuse
1 :	1 :	$\sqrt{2}$
x :	x :	$x\sqrt{2}$

What does it mean that the sides of a 45–45–90 triangle are in a 1 : 1 : $\sqrt{2}$ ratio? It doesn't mean that they are actually 1, 1, or $\sqrt{2}$ (although that's a possibility). It means that the sides are some multiple of 1 : 1 : $\sqrt{2}$. For instance, they could be 2, 2, and $2\sqrt{2}$, or 5.5, 5.5, and $5.5\sqrt{2}$. In the last two cases, the number we multiplied the ratio by—either 2 or 5.5 —is called the "multiplier." Using a multiplier of has the same effect as doubling a recipe—each of the ingredients gets doubled. Of course you can also triple a recipe or multiply it by any other number, even a fraction.

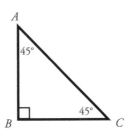

Given that the length of side *AB* is 5, what are the lengths of sides *BC* and *AC*?

Since *AB* is 5, we use the ratio 1 : 1 : $\sqrt{2}$ for sides *AB* : *BC* : *AC* to determine that the multiplier *x* is 5. We then find that the sides of the triangle have lengths 5 : 5 : $5\sqrt{2}$. Therefore, the length of side *BC* = 5, and the length of side *AC* = $5\sqrt{2}$. Using the same figure, let's discuss the following problem.

Given that the length of side *AC* is $\sqrt{18}$, what are the lengths of sides *AB* and *BC*?

Since the hypotenuse *AC* is $\sqrt{18} = x\sqrt{2}$, we find that $x = \sqrt{18} \div \sqrt{2} = \sqrt{9} = 3$. Thus, the sides *AB* and *BC* are each equal to *x*, or 3.

One reason that the 45–45–90 triangle is so important is that this triangle is exactly half of a square! That is, two 45–45–90 triangles put together make up a square. Thus, if you are given the diagonal of a square, you can use the 45–45–90 ratio to find the length of a side of the square.

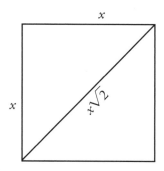

Check Your Skills

19. What is the area of a square with diagonal of 6?
20. What is the diagonal of a square with an area of 25?

Answers can be found on page 43–44.

Equilateral Triangles and the 30–60–90 Triangle

An equilateral triangle is one in which all three sides (and all three angles) are equal. Each angle of an equilateral triangle is 60° (because all 3 angles must sum to 180°). A close relative of the equilateral triangle is the 30–60–90 triangle. Notice that two of these triangles, when put together, form an equilateral triangle:

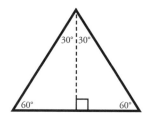

EQUILATERAL TRIANGLE

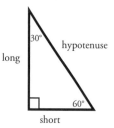

30–60–90 TRIANGLE

The lengths of the legs of every 30–60–90 triangle have the following ratio, which you must memorize:

30°	→	60°	→	90°
short leg		long leg		hypotenuse
1	:	$\sqrt{3}$	:	2
x	:	$x\sqrt{3}$	:	$2x$

    Given that the short leg of a 30–60–90 triangle has a length of 6, what are the lengths of the long leg and the hypotenuse?

The short leg, which is opposite the 30 degree angle, is 6. We use the ratio $1 : \sqrt{3} : 2$ to determine that the multiplier x is 6. We then find that the sides of the triangle have lengths 6: $6\sqrt{3}$: 12. The long leg measures $6\sqrt{3}$ and the hypotenuse measures 12.

    Given that an equilateral triangle has a side of length 10, what is its height?

Looking at the equilateral triangle above, we can see that the side of an equilateral triangle is the same as the hypotenuse of a 30–60–90 triangle. Additionally, the height of an equilateral triangle is the same as the long leg of a 30–60–90 triangle.

Since we are told that the hypotenuse is 10, we use the ratio $x : x\sqrt{3} : 2x$ to set $2x = 10$ and determine that the multiplier x is 5. We then find that the sides of the 30–60–90 triangle have lengths $5 : 5\sqrt{3} : 10$. Thus, the long leg has a length of $5\sqrt{3}$, which is the height of the equilateral triangle.

If you get tangled up on a 30–60–90 triangle, try to find the length of the short leg. The other legs will then be easier to figure out.

Check Your Skills

21. Quadrilateral *ABCD* (right) is composed of four 30–60–90 triangles. If *BD* = $10(\sqrt{3})$, what is the perimeter of *ABCD*?

22. Each side of the equilateral triangle below is 2. What is the height of the triangle?

Answers can be found on page 44.

Diagonals of Other Polygons

Right triangles are useful for more than just triangle problems. They are also helpful for finding the diagonals of other polygons, specifically squares, cubes, rectangles, and rectangular solids.

The diagonal of a square can be found using this formula:
   $d = s\sqrt{2}$, where s is a side of the square.
   This is also the face diagonal of a cube.

Alternatively, you can recall that any square can be divided into two 45–45–90 triangles and use the ratio $1 : 1 : \sqrt{2}$ to find the diagonal. You can also always use the Pythagorean Theorem.

   Given a square with a side of length 5, what is the length of the diagonal of the square?

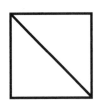

Using the formula $d = s\sqrt{2}$, we find that the length of the diagonal of the square is $5\sqrt{2}$.

The main diagonal of a cube can be found using this formula:
   $d = s\sqrt{3}$, where s is an edge of the cube.

What is the measure of an edge of a cube with a main diagonal of length $\sqrt{60}$?

Again, using the formula $d = s\sqrt{3}$, we solve as follows:

$$\sqrt{60} = s\sqrt{3} \rightarrow s = \frac{\sqrt{60}}{\sqrt{3}} = \sqrt{20}$$

Thus, the length of the edge of the cube is $\sqrt{20}$.

To find the diagonal of a rectangle, you must know EITHER the length and the width OR one dimension and the proportion of one to the other.

We will use the rectangle to the left for the next two problems.

If the rectangle above has a length of 12 and a width of 5, what is the length of the diagonal?

Using the Pythagorean Theorem, we solve:

$$5^2 + 12^2 = c^2 \rightarrow 25 + 144 = c^2 \rightarrow c = 13$$

The diagonal length is 13.

If the rectangle above has a width of 6, and the ratio of the width to the length is 3 : 4, what is the diagonal?

In this problem, we can use the ratio to find the value of the length. Using the ratio of 3 : 4 given in this problem, we find that the length is 8. Then we can use the Pythagorean Theorem. Alternatively, we can recognize that this is a 6–8–10 triangle. Either way, we find that the diagonal length is 10.

Check Your Skills

23. What is the diagonal of the rectangle above?

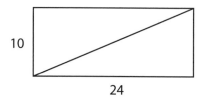

24. If the rectangle above has a perimeter of 6, what is its diagonal?

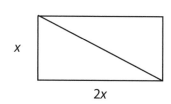

Answers can be found on page 44.

Check Your Skills Answers

1. **No:** If the two known sides of the triangle are 5 and 19, then the third side of the triangle cannot have a length of 13, because that would violate the rule that any two sides of a triangle must add up to greater than the third side. $5 + 13 = 18$, and $18 < 19$.

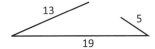

No possible triangle with these lengths.

2. **9 < third side < 25:** If the two known sides of the triangle are 8 and 17, then the third side must be less than the sum of the other 2 sides. $8 + 17 = 25$, so the third side must be less than 25. The third side must also be greater than the difference of the other two sides. $17 - 8 = 9$, so the third side must be greater than 9. That means that $9 <$ third side < 25.

3. **65°:** The internal angles of a triangle must add up to 180°, so we know that $40 + 75 + x = 180$. Solving for x gives us $x = 65°$.

4. **65°:** The 3 internal angles of the triangle must add up to 180°, so $50 + x + x = 180$. That means that $2x = 130$, and $x = 65$.

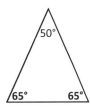

5. **$x = 70°$, $y = 80°$:** In order to determine the missing angles of the triangle, we need to do a little work with the picture. We can figure out the value of x, because straight lines have a degree measure of 180, so $110 + x = 180$, which means $x = 70$.

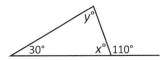

That means our picture looks like this:

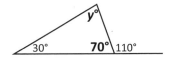

Now we can find y, because $30 + 70 + y = 180$. Solving for y gives us $y = 80$.

6. **80°:** In this triangle, two sides have the same length, which means this triangle is isosceles. We also know that the two angles opposite the two equal sides will also be equal. That means that x must be 80.

7. **4:** In this triangle, two angles are equal, which means this triangle is isosceles. We also know that the two sides opposite the equal angles must also be equal, so *x* must equal 4.

8. **110°:** This triangle is isosceles, because two sides have the same length. That means that the angles opposite the equal sides must also be equal.

That means our triangle really looks like this:

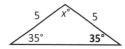

Now we can find *x*, because we know 35 + 35 + *x* = 180. Solving for *x* gives us *x* = 110.

9. **25:**

To find the perimeter of the triangle, we add up all three sides. 5 + 8 + 12 = 25, so the perimeter is 25.

10. **16:** To find the perimeter of the triangle, we need the lengths of all three sides. This is an isosceles triangle, because two angles are equal. That means that the sides opposite the equal angles must also be equal. So our triangle looks like this:

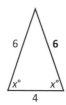

So the perimeter is 6 + 6 + 4, which equals 16. The perimeter is 16.

11. **15:** The area of a triangle is $^1/_2 b \times h$. In the triangle shown, the base is 6 and the height is 5. So the area is $^1/_2(6) \times 5$, which equals 15.

12. **35:** In this triangle, the base is 10 and the height is 7. Remember that the height must be perpendicular to the base—it doesn't need to lie within the triangle. So the area is $^{1}/2(10) \times 7$, which equals 35. The area of the triangle is 35.

13. **6:** This is a right triangle, so we can use the Pythagorean Theorem to solve for the length of the third side. The hypotenuse is the side with length 10, so the formula is $(8)^2 + b^2 = (10)^2$. $64 + b^2 = 100$. $b^2 = 36$, which means $b = 6$. So the third side of the triangle has a length of 6. Alternatively, you could recognize that this triangle is one of the Pythagorean triplets—a 6–8–10 triangle, which is just a doubled 3–4–5 triangle.

14. **13:** This is a right triangle, so we can use the Pythagorean Theorem to solve for the length of the third side. The hypotenuse is the unknown side, so the formula is $(5)^2 + (12)^2 = c^2$. $25 + 144 = c^2$. $c^2 = 169$, which means $c = 13$. So the third side of the triangle has a length of 13. Alternatively, you could recognize that this triangle is one of the Pythagorean triplets—a 5–12–13 triangle.

15. **length = 3, area = 6:** This is a right triangle, so we can use the Pythagorean Theorem to solve for the third side, or alternatively recognize that this is a 3–4–5 triangle. Either way, the result is the same: The length of the third side is 3.

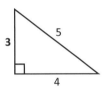

Now we can find the are of the triangle. Area of a triangle is $^{1}/2b \times h$, so the area of this triangle is $^{1}/2(3) \times (4)$, which equals 6. The area of the triangle is 6.

16. $\sqrt{2}$: Apply the Pythagorean theorem directly, substituting 1 for A and B,

$$1^2 + 1^2 = C^2$$
$$2 = C^2$$
$$C = \sqrt{2}$$

17. $\sqrt{3}$: Apply the Pythagorean theorem directly, substituting 1 for A and 2 for C,

$$1^2 + B^2 = 2^2$$
$$1 + B^2 = 4$$
$$B^2 = 3$$
$$B = \sqrt{3}$$

18. **3 and 4:** Since an isosceles triangle has two equal sides, the third side must be equal to one of the two named sides.

19. **18:** The ratio of the diagonal of a square to a side of the same square is $\sqrt{2}:1$, or $\sqrt{2}x:x$. Apply that to the square described above. In this instance, since $\sqrt{2}x:6$, x must be $\dfrac{6}{\sqrt{2}}$. Don't bother to simplify that

ungainly result, you're just going to square it anyway to get the area— $\left(\dfrac{6}{\sqrt{2}}\right)^2 = \dfrac{36}{2} = 18$.

20. **$5\sqrt{2}$**: The ratio of the diagonal of a square to a side of the same square is $\sqrt{2}:1$, or $\sqrt{2}x:x$. Apply that to the square described above. In this instance, since $x = 5$, the diagonal equals $5\sqrt{2}$.

21. **40**: The long diagonal BD is the sum of two long legs of the 30–60–90 triangle, so each long leg is $5\sqrt{3}$. The leg–leg–hypotenuse ratio of a 30–60–90 triangle is $x : x\sqrt{3} : 2x$, which means that $5\sqrt{3} = x\sqrt{3}$. Therefore $x = 5$, so the length of the short leg is 5 and the length of the hypotenuse is 10. Since the perimeter of the figure is the sum of four hypotenuses, the perimeter of this figure is 40.

22. **$\sqrt{3}$**: The line along which the height is measured in the figure above bisects the equilateral triangle, creating two identical 30–60–90 triangles, each with a base of 1. The base of each of these triangles is the short leg of a 30–60–90 triangle. Since the leg : leg : hypotenuse ratio of a 30–60–90 triangle is $1 : \sqrt{3} : 2$, the long leg of each 30–60–90 triangle, and the height of the equilateral triangle, is $\sqrt{3}$.

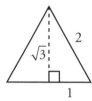

23. **26**: The diagonal of the rectangle is the hypotenuse of a right triangle whose legs are the length and width of the rectangle. In this case that means that the legs of the right triangle are 10 and 24. Plug these leg lengths into the Pythagorean Theorem:

$$A^2 + B^2 = C^2$$
$$10^2 + 24^2 = C^2$$
$$C^2 = 100 + 576 = 676$$
$$C = \sqrt{676} = 26$$

Alternatively, you could recognize the 10 : 24 : 26 triangle (a multiple of the more common 5 : 12 : 13 triangle), and save yourself the trouble and risk of error that comes with squaring 24 and taking the square root of 676.

24. **$\sqrt{5}$**: The perimeter of a rectangle is 2(length + width). In this case, that means $2(x + 2x)$, or $6x$. We are told the perimeter equals 6, so $6x = 6$, and $x = 1$. Therefore the length ($2x$) is 2 and the width (x) is 1. The diagonal of the rectangle is the hypotenuse of a right triangle whose legs are the length and width of the rectangle. Plug the leg lengths into the Pythagorean theorem:

$$A^2 + B^2 = C^2$$
$$1^2 + 2^2 = C^2$$
$$C^2 = 1 + 4 = 5$$
$$C = \sqrt{5}$$

Problem Set (Note: Figures are not drawn to scale.)

1.   A square is bisected into two equal triangles (see figure). If the length of *BD* is $16\sqrt{2}$ inches, what is the area of the square?

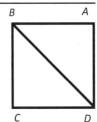

2.   Beginning in Town A, Biker Bob rides his bike 10 miles west, 3 miles north, 5 miles east, and then 9 miles north, to Town B. How far apart are Town A and Town B? (Ignore the curvature of the earth.)

3.   Now in Town B, Biker Bob walks due west, and then straight north to Town C. If Town B and Town C are 26 miles apart, and Biker Bob went 10 miles west, how many miles north did he go? (Again, ignore the curvature of the earth.)

4.   The longest side of an isosceles right triangle measures $20\sqrt{2}$. What is the area of the triangle?

5.   A square field has an area of 400 square meters. Posts are set at all corners of the field. What is the longest distance between any two posts?

6.   In Triangle *ABC*, *AD = DB = DC* (see figure). Given that angle *DCB* is 60° and angle *ACD* is 20°, what is the measure of angle *x*?

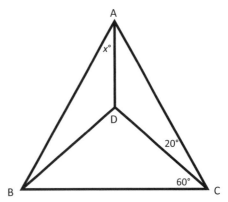

7.   Two sides of a triangle are 4 and 10. If the third side is an integer *x*, how many possible values are there for *x*?

8.   Jack makes himself a clay box in the shape of a cube, the edges of which are 4 inches long. What is the longest object he could fit inside the box (i.e., what is the diagonal of the cube)?

9.   What is the area of an equilateral triangle whose sides measure 8 cm long?

10.   The points of a six-pointed star consist of six identical equilateral triangles, with each side 4 cm (see figure). What is the area of the entire star, including the center?

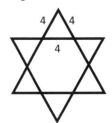

11.   What is *x* in the diagram below?

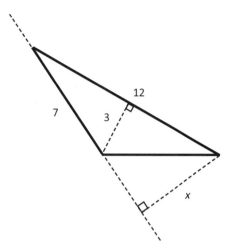

12.

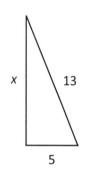

Column A
x

Column B
12

13.

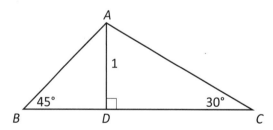

Column A

The perimeter of triangle *ABC* above

Column B

5

14.

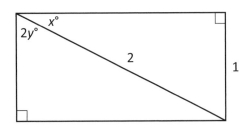

Column A	**Column B**
x	y

1. **256 square units:** The diagonal of a square is $s\sqrt{2}$; therefore, the side length of square ABCD is 16. The area of the square is s^2, or $16^2 = 256$.

2. **13 miles:** If you draw a rough sketch of the path Biker Bob takes, as shown to the right, you can see that the direct distance from A to B forms the hypotenuse of a right triangle. The short leg (horizontal) is $10 - 5 = 5$ miles, and the long leg (vertical) is $9 + 3 = 12$ miles. Therefore, you can use the Pythagorean Theorem to find the direct distance from A to B:

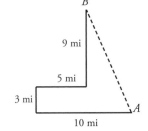

$$5^2 + 12^2 = c^2$$
$$25 + 144 = c^2$$
$$c^2 = 169 \quad \text{You might recognize the common right triangle:}$$
$$c = 13 \quad 5\text{–}12\text{–}13.$$

3. **24 miles:** If you draw a rough sketch of the path Biker Bob takes, as shown to the right, you can see that the direct distance from B to C forms the hypotenuse of a right triangle.

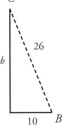

$$10^2 + b^2 = 26^2 \qquad \text{To find the square root of 576, you may find}$$
$$100 + b^2 = 676 \qquad \text{it helpful to prime factor it first:}$$
$$b^2 = 576 \qquad\qquad 576 = 2^6 \times 3^2$$
$$b = 24 \qquad\qquad \text{Therefore, } \sqrt{576} = 2^3 \times 3 = 24.$$

You might recognize this as a multiple of the common 5–12–13 triangle.

4. **200:** An isosceles right triangle is a 45–45–90 triangle, with sides in the ratio of $1 : 1 : \sqrt{2}$. If the longest side, the hypotenuse, measures $20\sqrt{2}$, the two other sides each measure 20. Therefore, the area of the triangle is:

$$A = \frac{b \times h}{2} = \frac{20 \times 20}{2} = 200$$

5: **$20\sqrt{2}$:** The longest distance between any two posts is the diagonal of the field. If the area of the field is 400 square meters, then each side must measure 20 meters. Diagonal $= d = s\sqrt{2}$, so $d = 20\sqrt{2}$.

6. **10:** If $AD = DB = DC$, then the three triangular regions in this figure are all isosceles triangles. Therefore, we can fill in some of the missing angle measurements as shown to the right. Since we know that there are 180° in the large triangle ABC, we can write the following equation:

$$x + x + 20 + 20 + 60 + 60 = 180$$
$$2x + 160 = 180$$
$$x = 10$$

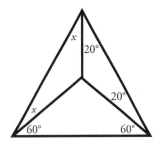

7. **7:** If two sides of a triangle are 4 and 10, the third side must be greater than 10 – 4 and smaller than 10 + 4. Therefore, the possible values for x are {7, 8, 9, 10, 11, 12, and 13}. You can draw a sketch to convince yourself of this result:

8. **4√3:** The diagonal of a cube with side s is $s\sqrt{3}$. Therefore, the longest object Jack could fit inside the box would be $4\sqrt{3}$ inches long.

9. **16√3:** Draw in the height of the triangle (see figure). If triangle ABC is an equilateral triangle, and ABD is a right triangle, then ABD is a 30–60–90 triangle. Therefore, its sides are in the ratio of $1:\sqrt{3}:2$. If the hypotenuse is 8, the short leg is 4, and the long leg is $4\sqrt{3}$. This is the height of triangle ABC. Find the area of triangle ABC with the formula for area of a triangle:

$$A = \frac{b \times h}{2} = \frac{8 \times 4\sqrt{3}}{2} = 16\sqrt{3}$$

Alternatively, you can apply the formula $A = \dfrac{S^2\sqrt{3}}{4}$, yielding $A = \dfrac{8^2\sqrt{3}}{4} = \dfrac{64\sqrt{3}}{4} = 16\sqrt{3}$.

10. **48√3 cm²:** We can think of this star as a large equilateral triangle with sides 12 cm long, and three additional smaller equilateral triangles with sides 4 inches long. Using the same 30–60–90 logic we applied in problem #9, we can see that the height of the larger equilateral triangle is $6\sqrt{3}$, and the height of the smaller equilateral triangle is $2\sqrt{3}$.

Therefore, the areas of the triangles are as follows:

Large triangle: $A = \dfrac{b \times h}{2} = \dfrac{12 \times 6\sqrt{3}}{2} = 36\sqrt{3}$

Small triangles: $A = \dfrac{b \times h}{2} = \dfrac{4 \times 2\sqrt{3}}{2} = 4\sqrt{3}$

The total area of three smaller triangles and one large triangle is:
$36\sqrt{3} + 3(4\sqrt{3}) = 48\sqrt{3}$ cm².

Alternatively, you can apply the formula $A = \dfrac{S^2\sqrt{3}}{4}$.

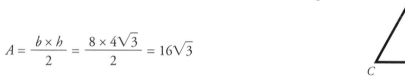

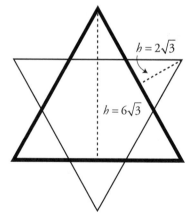

Large triangle: $A = \dfrac{12^2\sqrt{3}}{4} = \dfrac{144\sqrt{3}}{4} = 36\sqrt{3}.$

Small triangle: $A = \dfrac{4^2\sqrt{3}}{4} = \dfrac{16\sqrt{3}}{4} = 4\sqrt{3}.$

Then add the area of the large triangle and the area of three smaller triangles, as above.

11. **36/7:** We can calculate the area of the triangle, using the side of length 12 as the base:

$(1/2)(12)(3) = 18$

Next, we use the side of length 7 as the base and write the equation for the area:

$(1/2)(7)(x) = 18$

Now solve for x, the unknown height.

$7x = 36$

$x = 36/7$

You could also solve this problem using the Pythagorean Theorem, but the process is *much* harder.

12. **D:** Although this appears to be a 5 : 12 : 13 triangle, we do not know that it a right triangle. There is no "right triangle" symbol in the diagram. Remember, Don't Trust The Picture! Below are a couple of possible triangles:

13. **A:** Although there seems to be very little information here, the two small triangles that comprise *ABC* may seem familiar. First, fill in the additional angles in the diagram.

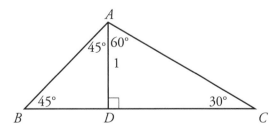

With the additional angles filled in, it is clear that the two smaller triangles are special right triangles: a 45–45–90 triangle and a 30–60–90 triangle. We know the ratios of the side lengths for each of these triangles. For a 45–45–90 triangle the ratio is $x : x : x\sqrt{2}$. In this diagram, the value of x is 1 (side *AD*), so *BD* is 1 and *AB* is $\sqrt{2}$.

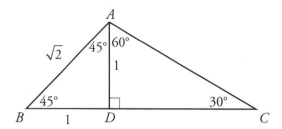

For a 30–60–90 triangle, the ratio is $x : x\sqrt{3} : 2x$. In this diagram, x is 1 (side AD), so CD is $\sqrt{3}$ and AC is 2.

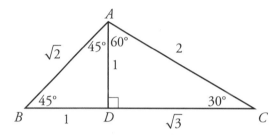

Now we can calculate the perimeter of triangle ABC.

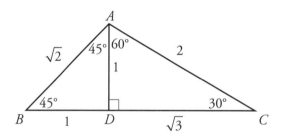

Column A	**Column B**
The perimeter of triangle ABC above = $\mathbf{1 + 2 + \sqrt{2} + \sqrt{3}}$	5

No we need to compare this sum to 5. A good approximation of $\sqrt{2}$ is 1.4 and a good approximation of $\sqrt{3}$ is 1.7.

Column A	**Column B**
$1 + 2 + \sqrt{2} + \sqrt{3} \approx$ $1 + 2 + 1.4 + 1.7 = \mathbf{5.1}$	5

14. **C:** The diagonal of the rectangle is the hypotenuse of a right triangle whose legs are the length and width of the rectangle. In this case we are given the width and diagonal. Plug those into the Pythagorean Theorem to determine the length:

*Manhattan*GRE*Prep
the new standard

$$A^2 + B^2 = C^2$$
$$1^2 + B^2 = 2^2$$
$$1 + B^2 = 4$$
$$B^2 = 3$$
$$B = \sqrt{3}$$

Plug this value into the diagram.

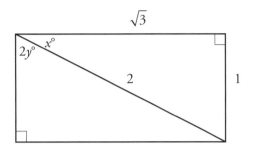

The key to this question is recognizing that each of the triangles are 30–60–90 triangles. Any time you see a right triangle and one of the sides has a length of $\sqrt{3}$ or a multiple of $\sqrt{3}$, you should check to see if it is a 30–60–90 triangle. Another clue is a right triangle in which the hypotenuse is twice the length of one of the sides.

Now, in addition to the side lengths, you can fill in the values of the angles in this diagram. Angle x is opposite the short leg, which means it has a degree measure of 30. Similarly, $2y$ is opposite the long leg, which means it has a degree measure of 60.

$$2y = 60$$
$$y = 30$$

Column A	**Column B**
$x = \mathbf{30}$	$y = \mathbf{30}$

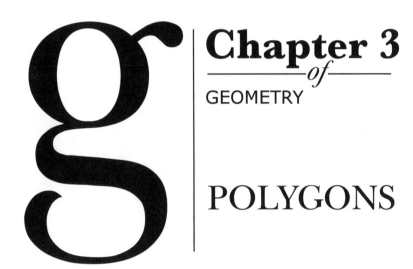

Chapter 3

of

GEOMETRY

POLYGONS

In This Chapter . . .

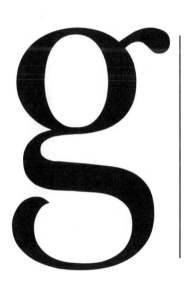

POLYGONS

Polygons are a very familiar sight on the GRE. As you saw in the last chapter, many questions about triangles will often involve other polygons, most notably quadrilaterals. Mastery of polygons will ultimately involve understanding the basic properties, such as perimeter and area, and will also involve the ability to distinguish polygons from other shapes in diagrams that include other polygons or circles.

A polygon is defined as a closed shape formed by line segments. The polygons tested on the GRE include the following:

- Three-sided shapes (Triangles)
- Four-sided shapes (Quadrilaterals)
- Other polygons with *n* sides (where *n* is five or more)

This section will focus on polygons of four or more sides. In particular, the GRE emphasizes quadrilaterals—four-sided polygons—squares, rectangles, parallelograms, and trapezoids.

Polygons are two-dimensional shapes—they lie in a plane. The GRE tests your ability to work with different measurements associated with polygons. The measurements you must be adept with are (1) interior angles, (2) perimeter, and (3) area.

The GRE also tests your knowledge of three-dimensional shapes formed from polygons, particularly rectangular solids and cubes. The measurements you must be adept with are (1) surface area and (2) volume.

Quadrilaterals: An Overview

The most common polygon tested on the GRE, aside from the triangle, is the quadrilateral (any four-sided polygon). Almost all GRE polygon problems involve the special types of quadrilaterals shown below.

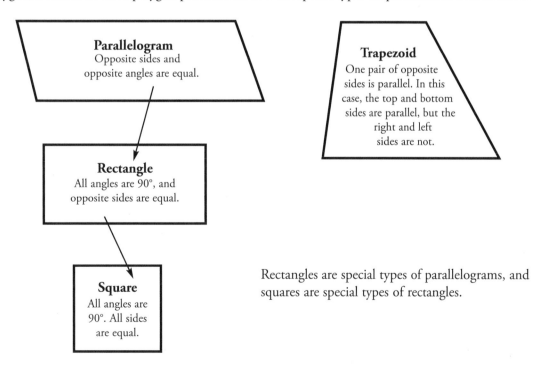

Parallelogram
Opposite sides and opposite angles are equal.

Trapezoid
One pair of opposite sides is parallel. In this case, the top and bottom sides are parallel, but the right and left sides are not.

Rectangle
All angles are 90°, and opposite sides are equal.

Square
All angles are 90°. All sides are equal.

Rectangles are special types of parallelograms, and squares are special types of rectangles.

Polygons and Interior Angles

The sum of the interior angles of a given polygon depends on the **number of sides in the polygon**. The following chart displays the relationship between the type of polygon and the sum of its interior angles.

The sum of the interior angles of a polygon follows a specific pattern that depends on n, the number of sides that the polygon has. This sum is always 180° times 2 less than n (the number of sides), because the polygon can be cut into $(n - 2)$ triangles, each of which contains 180°.

Polygon	# of Sides	Sum of Interior Angles
Triangle	3	180°
Quadrilateral	4	360°
Pentagon	5	540°
Hexagon	6	720°

This pattern can be expressed with the following formula:

$$(n - 2) \times 180 = \text{Sum of Interior Angles of a Polygon}$$

If you forget this formula, you can always say "okay, a triangle has 180°, a rectangle has 360°," and so on.

Since this polygon has four sides, the sum of its interior angles is $(4 - 2)180 = 2(180) = 360°$.

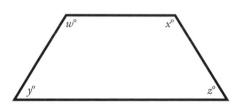

Alternatively, note that a quadrilateral can be cut into two triangles by a line connecting opposite corners. Thus, the sum of the angles = 2(180) = 360°.

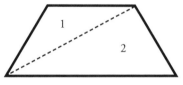

If a polygon has six sides, as in the figure below, the sum of its interior angles would be $(6 - 2)180 = 4(180) = 720°$.

Alternatively, note that a hexagon can be cut into four triangles by three lines connecting corners.

Thus, the sum of the angles = 4(180) = 720°.

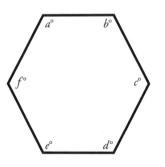

By the way, the corners of polygons are also known as vertices (singular: vertex).

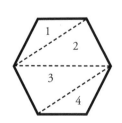

Check Your Skills

1. What is the sum of the interior angles of an octagon (eight-sided polygon)?
2. A regular polygon is a polygon in which every line is of equal length and every interior angle is equal. What is the degree measure of each interior angle in a regular hexagon (six-sided polygon)?

Answers can be found on page 67.

Polygons and Perimeter

The perimeter refers to the distance around a polygon, or the sum of the lengths of all the sides. The amount of fencing needed to surround a yard would be equivalent to the perimeter of that yard (the sum of all the sides).

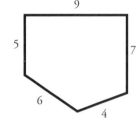

The perimeter of the pentagon to the right is:
9 + 7 + 4 + 6 + 5 = **31**.

Check Your Skills

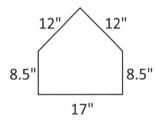

3. The figure above represents a standard baseball home plate. What is the perimeter of this figure?

Answers can be found on page 67.

Polygons and Area

The area of a polygon refers to the space inside the polygon. Area is measured in square units, such as cm^2 (square centimeters), m^2 (square meters), or ft^2 (square feet). For example, the amount of space that a garden occupies is the area of that garden.

On the GRE, there are two polygon area formulas you MUST know:

1) Area of a TRIANGLE $= \dfrac{\textbf{Base} \times \textbf{Height}}{\textbf{2}}$

The base refers to the bottom side of the triangle. The height ALWAYS refers to a line that is perpendicular (at a 90° angle) to the base.

In this triangle, the base is 6 and the height (perpendicular to the base) is 8. The area = (6 × 8) ÷ 2 = 48 ÷ 2 = 24.

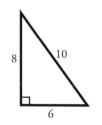

In this triangle, the base is 12, but the height is not shown. Neither of the other two sides of the triangle is perpendicular to the base. In order to find the area of this triangle, we would first need to determine the height, which is represented by the dotted line.

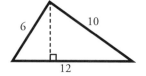

2) Area of a RECTANGLE = **Length × Width**

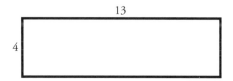

The length of this rectangle is 13, and the width is 4. Therefore, the area = 13 × 4 = 52.

The GRE will occasionally ask you to find the area of a polygon more complex than a simple triangle or rectangle. The following formulas can be used to find the areas of other types of quadrilaterals:

3) Area of a TRAPEZOID = $\dfrac{(\textbf{Base}_1 + \textbf{Base}_2) \times \textbf{Height}}{2}$

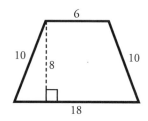

Note that the height refers to a line perpendicular to the two bases, which are parallel. (You often have to draw in the height, as in this case.) In the trapezoid shown, base₁ = 18, base₂ = 6, and the height = 8. The area = (18 + 6) × 8 ÷ 2 = 96. Another way to think about this is to take the *average* of the two bases and multiply it by the height.

4) Area of any PARALLELOGRAM = **Base × Height**

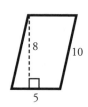

Note that the height refers to the line perpendicular to the base. (As with the trapezoid, you often have to draw in the height.) In the parallelogram shown, the base = 5 and the height = 8. Therefore, the area is 5 × 8 = 40.

Although these formulas are very useful to memorize for the GRE, you may notice that all of the above shapes can actually be divided into some combination of rectangles and right triangles. Therefore, if you forget the area formula for a particular shape, simply cut the shape into rectangles and right triangles, and then find the areas of these individual pieces. For example:

This trapezoid...   can be cut...   into 2 right triangles and 1 rectangle.

3 Dimensions: Surface Area

The GRE tests two particular three-dimensional shapes formed from polygons: the rectangular solid and the cube. Note that a cube is just a special type of rectangular solid.

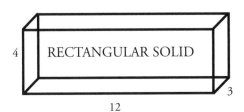

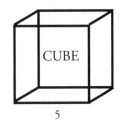

The surface area of a three-dimensional shape is the amount of space on the surface of that particular object. For example, the amount of paint that it would take to fully cover a rectangular box could be determined by finding the surface area of that box. As with simple area, surface area is measured in square units such as inches^2 (square inches) or ft^2 (square feet).

> **Surface Area = the SUM of the areas of ALL of the faces**

Both a rectangular solid and a cube have **six faces**.

To determine the surface area of a rectangular solid, you must find the area of each face. Notice, however, that in a rectangular solid, the front and back faces have the same area, the top and bottom faces have the same area, and the two side faces have the same area. In the solid above, the area of the front face is equal to $12 \times 4 = 48$. Thus, the back face also has an area of 48. The area of the bottom face is equal to $12 \times 3 = 36$. Thus, the top face also has an area of 36. Finally, each side face has an area of $3 \times 4 = 12$. Therefore, the surface area, or the sum of the areas of all six faces equals $48(2) + 36(2) + 12(2) = 192$.

To determine the surface area of a cube, you only need the length of one side. We can see from the cube above that a cube is made of six square surfaces. First, find the area of one face: $5 \times 5 = 25$. Then, multiply by six to account for all of the faces: $6 \times 25 = 150$.

Check Your Skills

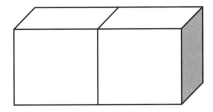

4. The figure to the left shows two wooden cubes joined to form a rectangular solid. If each cube has a surface area of 24, what is the surface area of the resulting rectangular solid?

Answers can be found on page 67.

3 Dimensions: Volume

The volume of a three-dimensional shape is the amount of "stuff" it can hold. For example, the amount of liquid that a rectangular milk carton holds can be determined by finding the volume of the carton. Volume is measured in cubic units such as inches^3 (cubic inches) or ft^3 (cubic feet).

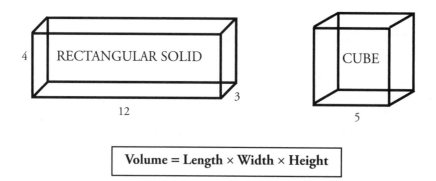

$$\boxed{\textbf{Volume = Length} \times \textbf{Width} \times \textbf{Height}}$$

By looking at the rectangular solid above, we can see that the length is 12, the width is 3, and the height is 4. Therefore, the volume is $12 \times 3 \times 4 = 144$.

In a cube, all three of the dimensions—length, width, and height—are identical. Therefore, knowing the measurement of just one side of the cube is sufficient to find the volume. In the cube above, the volume is $5 \times 5 \times 5 = 125$.

Check Your Skills

5. The volume of a rectangular solid with length 8, width 6, and height 4 is how many times the volume of a rectangular solid with length 4, width 3, and height 2?

Answers can be found on page 67.

Quadrilaterals

A quadrilateral is any figure with 4 sides. The GRE largely deals with one class of quadrilaterals known as **parallelograms.** A parallelogram is any 4 sided figure in which the opposite sides are parallel and equal and opposite angles are equal. This is an example of a parallelogram.

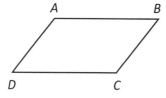

In this figure, sides *AB* and *CD* are parallel and have equal lengths, sides *AD* and *BC* are parallel and equal length, angles *ADC* and *ABC* are equal and angles *DAB* and *DCB* are equal.

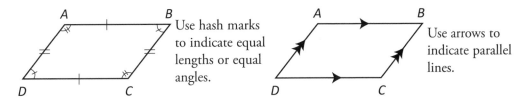

Use hash marks to indicate equal lengths or equal angles.

Use arrows to indicate parallel lines.

Any quadrilateral with two sets of opposite and equal sides is a parallelogram, as is any quadrilateral with two sets of opposite and equal angles.

An additional property of any parallelogram is that the diagonal will divide the parallelogram into 2 equal triangles.

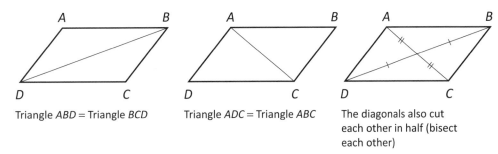

Triangle *ABD* = Triangle *BCD*

Triangle *ADC* = Triangle *ABC*

The diagonals also cut each other in half (bisect each other)

For any parallelogram, the perimeter is the sum of the lengths of all the sides and the area is equal to (base) × (height). With parallelograms, as with triangles, it is important to remember that the base and the height MUST be perpendicular to one another.

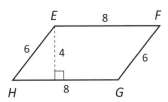

In this parallelogram, what is the perimeter, and what is the area? The perimeter is the sum of the sides, so it's 6 + 8 + 6 + 8 = 28. Alternatively, you can use one of the properties of parallelograms to calculate the perimeter in a different way. We know that parallelograms have two sets of equal sides. In this parallelogram, two of the sides have a length of 6, and two of the sides have a length of 8. So the perimeter equals 2 × 6 + 2 × 8. We can factor out a 2, and say that perimeter = 2 × (6 + 8) = 28.

To calculate the area, we need a base and a height. It might be tempting to say that the area is 6 × 8 = 48. But the two sides of this parallelogram are not perpendicular to each other. The dotted line drawn into the figure, however, is perpendicular to side *HG*. The area of parallelogram *EFGH* is 8 × 4 = 32.

Check Your Skills

6. What is the perimeter of the parallelogram?

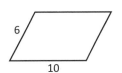

7. What is the area of the parallelogram?

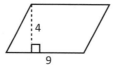

Answers can be found on page 67.

Rectangles

Rectangles are a specific type of parallelogram. Rectangles have all the same properties as parallelograms, with one additional property—all four internal angles of a rectangle are right angles. Additionally, with rectangles, we refer to one pair of sides as the length and one pair of sides as the width.

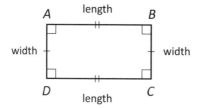

The formula for the perimeter of a rectangle is the same as for the perimeter of a parallelogram—either sum the lengths of the four sides or add the length and the width and multiply by 2.

The formula for the area of a rectangle is also the same as for the area of a parallelogram, but for any rectangle, the length and width are by definition perpendicular to each other, so you don't need a separate height. For this reason, the area of a rectangle is commonly expressed as (length) × (width).

Let's practice. For the following rectangle, find the perimeter and the area.

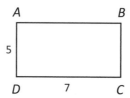

Let's start with the perimeter. Again, we can either fill in the missing sides and add them all up, or recognize that we have two sides with a length of 5 and two sides with a length of 7. Therefore, perimeter = 2 × (5 + 7), which equals 24. Alternatively, 5 + 5 + 7 + 7 also equals 24.

Now to find the area. The formula for area is (length) × (width). For the purposes of finding the area, it is irrelevant which side is the length and which side is the width. If we make *AD* the length and *DC* the width, then the area = (5) × (7) = 35. If, instead, we make *DC* the length and *AD* the width, then we have area = (7) × (5) = 35. The only thing that matters is that we choose two sides that are perpendicular to each other.

Check Your Skills

Find the area and perimeter of each rectangle.

8.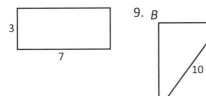

9.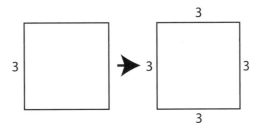

Answers can be found on pages 67–68.

Squares

One particular type of rectangle warrants mention—a square. A square is a rectangle in which the lengths of all four sides are equal. Everything that is true of rectangles is true of squares as well. What this means is that knowing only one side of a square is enough to determine the perimeter and area of a square.

For instance, if we have a square, and we know that the length of one of its sides is 3, we know that all 4 sides have a length of 3.

The perimeter of the square is $3 + 3 + 3 + 3$, which equals 12. Alternatively, once you know the length of one side of a square, you can multiply that length by 4 to find the perimeter. $3 \times 4 = 12$.

To find the area, we use the same formula as for a rectangle—Area = length × width. But, because the shape is a square, we know that the length and the width are equal. Therefore, we can say that the area of a square is Area = (side)^2. In this case, Area = $(3)^2 = 9$.

Maximum Area of Polygons

In some problems, the GRE may require you to determine the maximum or minimum area of a given figure. Whether the question is Discrete Quant or Quantitative Comparisons, following a few simple shortcuts can help you solve certain problems quickly.

Maximum Area of a Quadrilateral

Perhaps the best-known maximum–area problem is one which asks you to maximize the area of a *quadrilateral* (usually a rectangle) with a *fixed perimeter*. If a quadrilateral has a fixed perimeter, say, 36 inches, it can take a variety of shapes:

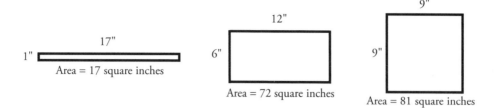

Area = 17 square inches

Area = 72 square inches

Area = 81 square inches

Of these figures, the one with the largest area is the square. This is a general rule: **Of all quadrilaterals with a given perimeter, the SQUARE has the largest area.** This is true even in cases involving non-integer lengths. For instance, of all quadrilaterals with a perimeter of 25 feet, the one with the largest area is a square with 25/4 = 6.25 feet per side.

This principle can also be turned around to yield the following corollary: **Of all quadrilaterals with a given area, the SQUARE has the minimum perimeter.**

Both of these principles can be generalized for *n* sides: a regular polygon with all sides equal (and pushed outward if necessary) will maximize area for a given perimeter and minimize perimeter for a given area.

Maximum Area of a Parallelogram or Triangle

Another common optimization problem involves maximizing the area of a *triangle or parallelogram with given side lengths.*

For instance, there are many triangles with two sides 3 and 4 units long. Imagine that the two sides of length 3 and 4 are on a hinge. The third side can have various lengths:

There are many corresponding parallelograms with two sides 3 and 4 units long:

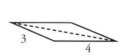 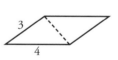

The area of a triangle is given by $A = \frac{1}{2}bh$, and the area of a parallelogram is given by $A = bh$. Because both of these formulas involve the perpendicular height *h*, the maximum area of each figure is achieved when the 3-unit side is perpendicular to the 4-unit side, so that the height is 3 units. All the other figures have lesser heights. (Note that in this case, the triangle of maximum area is the famous 3–4–5 right triangle.) If the sides are not perpendicular, then the figure is squished, so to speak.

The general rule is this: **if you are given two sides of a triangle or parallelogram, you can maximize the area by placing those two sides PERPENDICULAR to each other.**

Check Your Skills Answers

1. **1,080:** One way to calculate the sum of the interior angles of a polygon is by applying the formula $(n - 2)180 =$ Sum of the interior angles, where n is the number of sides. Substituting 8 for n yields:

$$\text{Sum of the interior angles} = (8 - 2)180$$
$$= (6)180$$
$$= 1,080$$

2. **120:** Since each interior angle is the same, we can determine the angle of any one by dividing the sum of the interior angles by 6 (the number of interior angles). Use the formula $(n - 2)180 =$ Sum of the interior angles, where n is the number of sides. Substituting 6 for n yields: Sum $= (4)180 = 720$. Divide 720 by 6 to get 120.

3. **58:** The sum of the five sides is 58". It simplest to arrange them as $12 + 12 + 17 + (8^{1}/_{2} + 8^{1}/_{2}) = 12 + 12 + 17 + 17 = 58$.

4. **40:** Since the surface area of a cube is 6 times the area of one face, each square face of each cube must have an area of 4. One face of each cube is lost when the two cubes are joined, so the total surface area of the figure will be the sum of the surface areas of both cubes minus the surface areas of the covered faces.

Each cube has surface area of 24, so the total surface area is 48. Subtract the surface area of each covered face (4). $48 - 2(4) = 40$.

5. **8:** The volume of a rectangular solid is the product of its three dimensions, length, width, and height.

$$8 \times 6 \times 4 = 192 \text{ and } 4 \times 3 \times 2 = 24$$

$\dfrac{192}{24} = 8$, so the volume of the larger cube is 8 times the volume of the smaller cube.

6. **32:** In parallelograms, opposite sides have equal lengths, so we know that two of the sides of the parallelogram have a length of 6 and two sides have a length of 10.

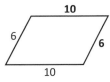

So the perimeter is $6 + 10 + 6 + 10$, which equals 32.

7. **36:** Area of a parallelogram is $b \times h$. In this parallelogram, the base is 9 and the height is 4, so the area is $(9) \times (4)$, which equals 36. The area of the parallelogram is 36.

8. **20, 21:** In rectangles, opposite sides have equal lengths, so our rectangle looks like this:

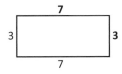

So the perimeter is 3 + 7 + 3 + 7, which equals 20. The area of a rectangle is $b \times h$, so the area is $(7) \times (3)$, which equals 21. So the perimeter is 20, and the area is 21.

9. **28, 48:** To find the area and perimeter of the rectangle, we need to know the length of either side *AB* or side *CD*. The diagonal of the rectangle creates a right triangle, so we can use the Pythagorean Theorem to find the length of side *CD*. Alternatively, we can recognize that triangle *ACD* is a 6–8–10 triangle, and thus the length of side *CD* is 8. Either way, our rectangle now looks like this:

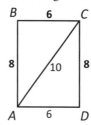

So the perimeter of the rectangle is 6 + 8 + 6 + 8, which equals 28. The area is $(6) \times (8)$, which equals 48.

Problem Set (Note: Figures are not drawn to scale.)

1. Frank the Fencemaker needs to fence in a rectangular yard. He fences in the entire yard, except for one 40-foot side of the yard. The yard has an area of 280 square feet. How many feet of fence does Frank use?

2. A pentagon has three sides with length x, and two sides with the length $3x$. If x is $\frac{2}{3}$ of an inch, what is the perimeter of the pentagon?

3. *ABCD* is a quadrilateral, with *AB* parallel to *CD* (see figure). *E* is a point between *C* and *D* such that *AE* represents the height of *ABCD*, and *E* is the midpoint of *CD*. If *AB* is 4 inches long, *AE* is 5 inches long, and the area of triangle *AED* is 12.5 square inches, what is the area of *ABCD*?

    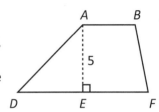

4. A rectangular tank needs to be coated with insulation. The tank has dimensions of 4 feet, 5 feet, and 2.5 feet. Each square foot of insulation costs $20. How much will it cost to cover the surface of the tank with insulation?

5. Triangle *ABC* (see figure) has a base of $2y$, a height of y, and an area of 49. What is y?

    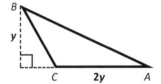

6. 40 percent of Andrea's living room floor is covered by a carpet that is 4 feet by 9 feet. What is the area of her living room floor?

7. If the perimeter of a rectangular flower bed is 30 feet, and its area is 44 square feet, what is the length of each of its shorter sides?

8. There is a rectangular parking lot with a length of $2x$ and a width of x. What is the ratio of the perimeter of the parking lot to the area of the parking lot, in terms of x?

9. A rectangular solid has a square base, with each side of the base measuring 4 meters. If the volume of the solid is 112 cubic meters, what is the surface area of the solid?

10. A swimming pool has a length of 30 meters, a width of 10 meters, and an average depth of 2 meters. If a hose can fill the pool at a rate of 0.5 cubic meters per minute, how many hours will it take the hose to fill the pool?

11. A Rubix cube has an edge 5 inches long. What is the ratio of the cube's surface area to its volume?

12. If the length of an edge of Cube A is one third the length of an edge of Cube B, what is the ratio of the volume of Cube A to the volume of Cube B?

13. *ABCD* is a square picture frame (see figure). *EFGH* is a square inscribed within *ABCD* as a space for a picture. The area of *EFGH* (for the picture) is equal to the area of the picture frame (the area of *ABCD* minus the area of *EFGH*). If *AB* = 6, what is the length of *EF*?

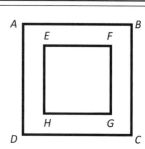

14. What is the maximum possible area of a quadrilateral with a perimeter of 80 centimeters?

15. What is the minimum possible perimeter of a quadrilateral with an area of 1,600 square feet?

16. What is the maximum possible area of a parallelogram with one side of length 2 meters and a perimeter of 24 meters?

17. What is the maximum possible area of a triangle with a side of length 7 units and another side of length 8 units?

18. The lengths of the two shorter legs of a right triangle add up to 40 units. What is the maximum possible area of the triangle?

19.

Column A	**Column B**
The surface area in square inches of a cube with edges of length 6.	The volume in cubic inches of a cube with edges of length 6.

20.

Column A	**Column B**
The total volume of 3 cubes with edges of length 2.	The total volume of 2 cubes with edges of length 3.

21.

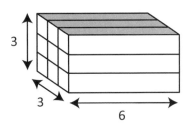

The large rectangular solid above is formed by binding together nine identical rectangular rods, as shown.

Column A

The combined surface area of four of the identical rectangular rods.

Column B

The surface area of the large rectangular solid.

1. **54 feet:** We know that one side of the yard is 40 feet long; let us call this the length. We also know that the area of the yard is 280 square feet. In order to determine the perimeter, we must know the width of the yard.

$$A = l \times w$$
$$280 = 40w$$
$$w = 280 \div 40 = 7 \text{ feet}$$

Frank fences in the two 7-foot sides and one of the 40-foot sides. $40 + 2(7) = 54$.

2. **6 inches:** The perimeter of a pentagon is the sum of its five sides: $x + x + x + 3x + 3x = 9x$. If x is 2/3 of an inch, the perimeter is $9(2/3)$, or 6 inches.

3. **35 in²:** If E is the midpoint of C, then $CE = DE = x$. We can determine the length of x by using what we know about the area of triangle AED.

$$A = \frac{b \times h}{2} \quad 12.5 = \frac{5x}{2}$$

$$25 = 5x$$
$$x = 5$$

Therefore, the length of CD is $2x$, or 10.

To find the area of the trapezoid, use the formula: $\quad A = \dfrac{b_1 + b_2}{2} \times h$

$$= \frac{4 + 10}{2} \times 5$$

$$= 35 \text{ in}^2$$

4. **$1,700:** To find the surface area of a rectangular solid, sum the individual areas of all six faces:

Top and Bottom:	$5 \times 4 \ = 20$	$\rightarrow$	$2 \times 20 \ = 40$
Side 1:	$5 \times 2.5 = 12.5$	$\rightarrow$	$2 \times 12.5 = 25$
Side 2:	$4 \times 2.5 = 10$	$\rightarrow$	$2 \times 10 \ = 20$

$$40 + 25 + 20 = 85 \text{ ft}^2$$

Covering the entire tank will cost $85 \times \$20 = \$1,700$.

5. **7:** The area of a triangle is equal to half the base times the height. Therefore, we can write the following relationship:

$$\frac{2y(y)}{2} = 49$$

$$y^2 = 49$$
$$y = 7$$

6. **90 ft²:** The area of the carpet is equal to $l \times w$, or 36 ft². Set up a percent table or a proportion to find the area of the whole living room floor:

$$\frac{40}{100} = \frac{36}{x}$$ Cross-multiply to solve.

$$40x = 3600$$
$$x = 90 \text{ ft}^2$$

7. **4:** Set up equations to represent the area and perimeter of the flower bed:

$$A = l \times w \qquad\qquad P = 2(l + w)$$

Then, substitute the known values for the variables A and P:

$$44 = l \times w \qquad\qquad 30 = 2(l + w)$$

Solve the two equations with the substitution method:

$$l = \frac{44}{w}$$

$$30 = 2(\frac{44}{w} + w)$$

$$30 = \frac{88}{w} + 2w$$ Multiply the entire equation by $\frac{w}{2}$.

$$15w = 44 + w^2$$

$$w^2 - 15w + 44 = 0$$ Solving the quadratic equation yields two solutions: 4 and 11. Since we are looking only for the length of the shorter side, the answer is 4.

$$(w - 11)(w - 4) = 0$$

$$w = \{4, 11\}$$

Alternatively, you can arrive at the correct solution by picking numbers. What length and width add up to 15 (half of the perimeter) and multiply to produce 44 (the area)? Some experimentation will demonstrate that the longer side must be 11 and the shorter side must be 4.

8. $\dfrac{3}{x}$: If the length of the parking lot is $2x$ and the width is x, we can set up a fraction to represent the ratio of the perimeter to the area as follows:

$$\frac{\text{perimeter}}{\text{area}} = \frac{2(2x + x)}{(2x)(x)} = \frac{6x}{2x^2} = \frac{3}{x}$$

9. **144 m²:** The volume of a rectangular solid equals (length) × (width) × (height). If we know that the length and width are both 4 meters long, we can substitute values into the formulas as shown:

$$112 = 4 \times 4 \times h$$
$$h = 7$$

To find the surface area of a rectangular solid, sum the individual areas of all six faces:

Top and Bottom:	$4 \times 4 = 16$	$\rightarrow$	$2 \times 16 = 32$
Sides:	$4 \times 7 = 28$	$\rightarrow$	$4 \times 28 = 112$

$$32 + 112 = 144 \, \text{m}^2$$

10. **20 hours:** The volume of the pool is (length) × (width) × (height), or $30 \times 10 \times 2 = 600$ cubic meters. Use a standard work equation, $RT = W$, where W represents the total work of 600 m³.

$0.5t = 600$
$\quad t = 1{,}200$ minutes   Convert this time to hours by dividing by 60: $1{,}200 \div 60 = 20$ hours.

11. $\dfrac{6}{5}$: To find the surface area of a cube, find the area of 1 face, and multiply that by 6: $6(5^2) = 150$. To find the volume of a cube, cube its edge length: $5^3 = 125$.

The ratio of the cube's surface area to its volume, therefore, is $\dfrac{150}{125}$, or $\dfrac{6}{5}$.

12. **1 to 27:** First, assign the variable x to the length of one side of Cube A. Then the length of one side of Cube B is $3x$. The volume of Cube A is x^3. The volume of Cube B is $(3x)^3$, or $27x^3$.

Therefore, the ratio of the volume of Cube A to Cube B is $\dfrac{x^3}{27x^3}$, or 1 to 27. You can also pick a number for the length of a side of Cube A and solve accordingly.

13. **3√2:** The area of the frame and the area of the picture sum to the total area of the image, which is 6^2, or 36. Therefore, the area of the frame and the picture are each equal to half of 36, or 18. Since $EFGH$ is a square, the length of EF is $\sqrt{18}$, or $3\sqrt{2}$.

14. **400 cm²:** The quadrilateral with maximum area for a given perimeter is a square, which has four equal sides. Therefore, the square that has a perimeter of 80 centimeters has sides of length 20 centimeters each. Since the area of a square is the side length squared, the area = (20 cm)(20 cm) = 400 cm².

15. **160 ft:** The quadrilateral with minimum perimeter for a given area is a square. Since the area of a square is the side length squared, we can solve the equation $x^2 = 1{,}600$ ft² for the side length x, yielding $x = 40$ ft. The perimeter, which is four times the side length, is (4)(40 ft) = 160 ft.

16. **20 m²:** If one side of the parallelogram is 2 meters long, then the opposite side must also be 2 meters long. We can solve for the unknown sides, which are equal in length, by writing an equation for the perimeter: $24 = 2(2) + 2x$, with x as the unknown side. Solving, we get $x = 10$ meters. The parallelogram with these dimensions and maximum area is a *rectangle* with 2-meter and 10-meter sides. Thus the maximum possible area of the figure is (2 m)(10 m) = 20 m².

17. **28 square units:** A triangle with two given sides has maximum area if these two sides are placed at right angles to each other. For this triangle, one of the given sides can be considered the base, and the other side can be considered the height (because they meet at a right angle). Thus we plug these sides into the

formula $A = \frac{1}{2}bh$: $A = \frac{1}{2}(7)(8) = 28$.

18. **200 square units:** You can think of a right triangle as half of a rectangle. Constructing this right triangle with legs adding to 40 is equivalent to constructing the rectangle with a perimeter of 80. Since the area of the triangle is half that of the rectangle, you can use the previously mentioned technique for maximizing the area of a rectangle: of all rectangles with a given perimeter, the *square* has the greatest area. The desired rectangle is thus a 20 by 20 square, and the right triangle has area (1/2)(20)(20) = 200 units.

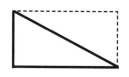

19. **C:** The surface area of a cube is 6 times e^2, where e *is* the length of each edge (that is, the surface area is the number of faces times the area of each face). Apply this formula to Column A.

Column A	**Column B**
The surface area in square inches of a cube with edges of length 6 = **6 × (6 × 6)**	The volume in cubic inches of a cube with edges of length 6.

The volume of a cube is e^3, where e is the length of each edge. Apply this formula to Column B.

Column A	**Column B**
6 × (6 × 6)	The volume in cubic inches of a cube with edges of length 6 = **6 × 6 × 6**

It is not generally the case that the volume of a cube in cubic units is equal to the surface area of the cube in square inches; they are only equal when the edge of the cube is of length 6.

20. **B:** The volume of a cube is e^3, where e is the length of each edge. Apply this formula to each column.

Column A	**Column B**
The total volume of 3 cubes with edges of length 2 = $3 \times (2^3) = \mathbf{24}$	The total volume of 2 cubes with edges of length 3 = $2 \times (3^3) = \mathbf{54}$

21. **A:** A rectangular solid has three pairs of opposing equal faces, each pair representing two of the dimensions of the solid (length × width; length × height; height × width). The total surface area of a rectangular solid is the sum of the surface areas of those three pairs of opposing sides.

According to the diagram, the dimensions of each rod must be 1 × 1 × 6. So each of the rods described in Column A has a surface area of
$$2(1 \times 1) + 2(1 \times 6) + 2(1 \times 6), \quad \text{or} \quad 2[(1 \times 1) + (1 \times 6) + (1 \times 6)]$$

That is, each rod has a total surface area of 26, and the four rods together have a surface area of $4 \times 26 = 104$.

<u>**Column A**</u>

The combined surface area of four
of the identical rectangular rods =
104

<u>**Column B**</u>

The surface area of the large
rectangular solid.

The large rectangular solid has a total surface area of
$2(3 \times 3) + 2(3 \times 6) + 2(3 \times 6)$, or 90.

<u>**Column A**</u>

104

<u>**Column B**</u>

The surface area of the large
rectangular solid = **90**

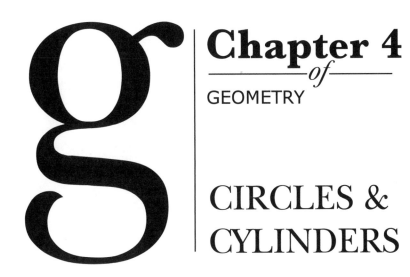

Chapter 4
of
GEOMETRY

CIRCLES & CYLINDERS

In This Chapter . . .

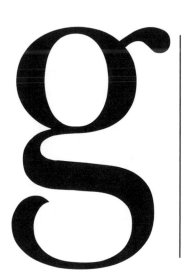

The Basic Elements of a Circle

A circle is a set of points that are all the same distance from a central point. By definition, every circle has a center. Although the center is not itself a point on the circle, it is nevertheless an important component of the circle. The **radius** of a circle is defined as the distance between the center of the circle and a point on the circle. The first thing to know about radii is that *any* line segment connecting the center of the circle (usually labeled *O*) and *any* point on the circle is a radius (usually labeled *r*). All radii in the same circle have the same length.

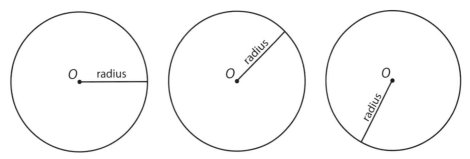

We'll discuss the other basic elements by dealing with a particular circle. Our circle will have a radius of 7, and we'll see what else we can figure out about the circle based on that one measurement. As you'll see, we'll be able to figure out quite a lot.

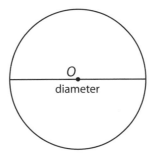

Once we know the radius, the next easiest piece to figure out is the **diameter.** The diameter passes through the center of a circle and connects 2 opposite points on the circle.

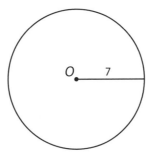

One way of thinking about the diameter (usually referred to as *d*) is that it is 2 radii laid end to end. The diameter will always be exactly twice the length of the radius. This relationship can be expressed as $d = 2r$. That means that our circle with radius 7 has a diameter of 14.

Now it's time for our next important measurement—the **circumference.** Circumference (usually referred to as *C*) is a measure of the distance around a circle. One way to think about circumference is that it's the perimeter of a circle.

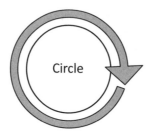

As it happens, there is a consistent relationship between the circumference and the diameter of any circle. If you were to divide the circumference by the diameter, you would always get the same number—3.14... (the number is actually a non-repeating decimal, so it's usually rounded to the hundredths place). You may be more familiar with this number as the Greek letter π (pi). To recap:

$$\frac{\text{circumference}}{\text{diameter}} = \pi. \text{ Or } \pi d = C.$$

In our circle with a diameter of 14, the circumference is $\pi(14) = 14\pi$. The vast majority of questions that involve circles and π will use the Greek letter and a decimal approximation. Suppose a question about our circle with radius 7 asked for the circumference. The correct answer would read 14π, rather than 43.96 (which is 14×3.14). It's worth mentioning that another very common way of expressing the circumference is that twice the radius times π also equals *C*, because the diameter is twice the radius. This relationship is commonly expressed as $C = 2\pi r$. As you prepare for the GRE, you should be comfortable with using either equation.

There is one more element of a circle that you'll need to be familiar with, and that is **area.** The area (usually referred to as *A*) is the space inside the circle.

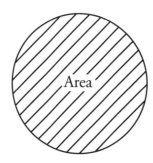

Once again, it turns out that there is a consistent relationship between the area of a circle and its diameter (and radius). If you know the radius of the circle, then the formula for the area is $A = \pi r^2$. For our circle of radius 7, the area is $\pi(7)^2 = 49\pi$. To recap, once we know the radius, we are able to determine the diameter, the circumference, and the area.

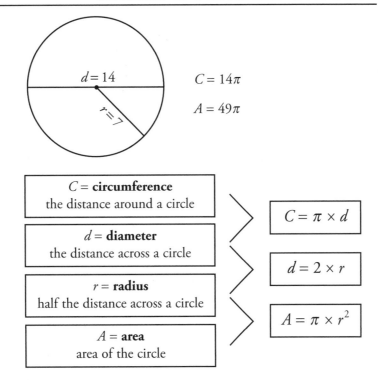

C = **circumference** the distance around a circle	$C = \pi \times d$
d = **diameter** the distance across a circle	$d = 2 \times r$
r = **radius** half the distance across a circle	$A = \pi \times r^2$
A = **area** area of the circle	

These relationships are true of any circle. What's more, if you know *any* of these values, you can determine the rest. In fact, the ability to use one element of a circle to determine another is one of the most important skills for answering questions about circles.

To demonstrate, we'll work through another circle, but this time we know that the area of the circle is 36π. Well, we know the formula for the area, so let's start by plugging this value into the formula.

$$36\pi = \pi r^2$$

Now we can solve for the radius by isolating r.

$36\pi = \pi r^2$ Divide by π

$36 = r^2$ Take the square root of both sides

$6 = r$

Now that we know the radius, we can simply multiply it by 2 to get the diameter, so our diameter is 12. Finally, to find the circumference, simply multiply the diameter by π, which gives us a circumference of 12π.

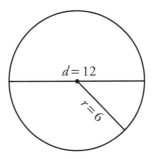

Check Your Skills

1. The radius of a circle is 7. What is the area? 49π
2. The circumference of a circle is 17π. What is the diameter?   17
3. The area of a circle is 25π. What is the circumference? 5γ

Answers can be found on page 89.

Sectors

Let's continue working with our circle that has an area of 36π. But now, let's cut it in half and make it a semi-circle. Any time you have a fractional portion of a circle, it's known as a **sector**.

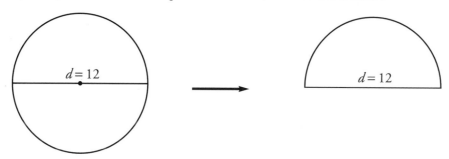

What effect does cutting the circle in half have on the basic elements of the circle? The diameter stays the same, as does the radius. But what happened to the area and the circumference? They're also cut in half. So the area of the semicircle is 18π and the circumference is 6π. When dealing with sectors, we call the portion of the circumference that remains the **arc length.** So the arc length of this sector is 6π.

In fact, this rule applies even more generally to circles. If, instead of cutting the circle in half, we had cut it into 1/4's, each piece of the circle would have 1/4 the area of the entire circle and 1/4 the circumference.

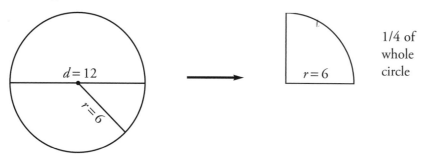

1/4 of whole circle

Now, on the GRE, you're unlikely to be told that you have 1/4th of a circle. There is one more basic element of circles that becomes relevant when you are dealing with sectors, and that is the **central angle.** The central angle of a sector is the degree measure between the two radii. Take a look at the quarter circle. Normally, there are 360° in a full circle. What is the degree measure of the angle between the 2 radii? The same thing that happens to area and circumference happens to the central angle. It is now 1/4th of 360°, which is 90°.

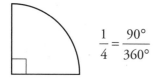

$$\frac{1}{4} = \frac{90°}{360°}$$

Let's see how we can use the central angle to determine sector area and arc length. For our next example, we will still use the circle with area 36π, but now the sector will have a central angle of 60°.

We need to figure out what fractional amount of the circle remains if the central angle is 60°. If 360° is the whole amount, and 60° is the part, then 60/360 is the fraction we're looking for. 60/360 reduces to 1/6. That means a sector with a central angle of 60° is 1/6th of the entire circle. If that's the case, then the sector area is 1/6 × (Area of circle) and arc length is 1/6 × (Circumference of circle). So:

Sector Area = 1/6 × (36π) = 6π

Arc Length = 1/6 × (12π) = 2π

$$\frac{1}{6} = \frac{60°}{360°} = \frac{\text{Sector Area}}{\text{Circle Area}} = \frac{\text{Arc Length}}{\text{Circumference}}$$

In our last example, we used the central angle to find what fractional amount of the circle the sector was. But any of the three properties of a sector (central angle, arc length and area) could be used if you know the radius.

Let's look at an example.

A sector has a radius of 9 and an area of 27π. What is the central angle of the sector?

We still need to determine what fractional amount of the circle the sector is. This time, however, we have to use the area to figure that out. We know the area of the sector, so if we can figure out the area of the whole circle, we can figure out what fractional amount the sector is.

We know the radius is 9, so we can calculate the area of the whole circle. Area = πr^2, so Area = $\pi(9)^2 = 81\pi$. $\frac{27\pi}{81\pi} = \frac{1}{3}$, so the sector is 1/3 of the circle. The full circle has a central angle of 360, so we can multiply that by 1/3. 1/3 × 360 = 120, so the central angle of the sector is 120°.

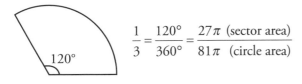

$$\frac{1}{3} = \frac{120°}{360°} = \frac{27\pi \ (\text{sector area})}{81\pi \ (\text{circle area})}$$

Let's recap what we know about sectors. Every question about sectors involves determining what fraction of the circle the sector is. That means that every question about sectors will provide you with enough info to calculate one of the following fractions:

$$\frac{\text{central angle}}{360} \qquad \frac{\text{sector area}}{\text{circle area}} \qquad \frac{\text{arc length}}{\text{circumference}}$$

Once you know any of those fractions, you know them all, and you can find the value of any piece of the sector or the original circle.

4π × .75   4r

Check Your Skills

4. A sector has a central angle of 270° and a radius of 2. What is the area of the sector?
5. A sector has an arc length of 4π and a radius of 3. What is the central angle of the sector?
6. A sector has an area of 40π and a radius of 10. What is the arc length of the sector?

Answers can be found on page 89.

Inscribed vs. Central Angles

Thus far, in dealing with arcs and sectors, we have referred to the concept of a **central angle**. A central angle is defined as an angle whose vertex lies at the center point of a circle. As we have seen, a central angle defines both an arc and a sector of a circle.

Another type of angle is termed an **inscribed angle**. An inscribed angle has its vertex on the circle itself. The following diagrams illustrate the difference between a central angle and an inscribed angle.

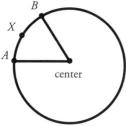
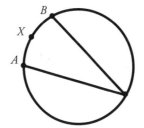
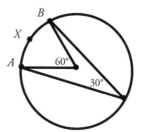

CENTRAL ANGLE   INSCRIBED ANGLE

Notice that, in the circle at the far right, there is a central angle and an inscribed angle, both of which intercept arc *AXB*. It is the central angle that defines the arc. That is, the arc is 60° (or one sixth of the complete 360° circle). **An inscribed angle is equal to half of the arc it intercepts**, in degrees. In this case, the inscribed angle is 30°, which is half of 60°.

Inscribed Triangles

Related to this idea of an inscribed angle is that of an **inscribed triangle**. A triangle is said to be inscribed in a circle if all of the vertices of the triangle are points on the circle.

Above right is a special case of the rule mentioned above (that an inscribed angle is equal to half of the arc it intercepts). In this case, the right angle (90°) lies opposite a semicircle, which is an arc that measures 180°.

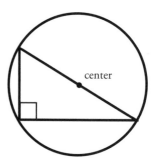

The important rule to remember is: **if one of the sides of an inscribed triangle is a DIAMETER of the circle, then the triangle MUST be a right triangle.**

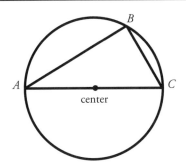

Conversely, any right triangle inscribed in a circle must have the diameter of the circle as one of its sides (thereby splitting the circle in half).

In the inscribed triangle to the left, triangle *ABC* must be a right triangle, since *AC* is a diameter of the circle.

Cylinders and Surface Area

Two circles and a rectangle combine to form a three-dimensional shape called a right circular cylinder (referred to from now on simply as a **cylinder**). The top and bottom of the cylinder are circles, while the middle of the cylinder is formed from a rolled-up rectangle, as shown in the diagram below:

In order to determine the surface area of a cylinder, sum the areas of the 3 surfaces: The area of each circle is πr^2, while the area of the rectangle is length × width. Looking at the figures on the right, we can see that the length of the rectangle is equal to the circumference of the circle ($2\pi r$), and the width of the rectangle is equal to the height of the cylinder (h). Therefore, the area of the rectangle is $2\pi r \times h$. To find the total surface area of a cylinder, add the area of the circular top and bottom, as well as the area of the rectangle that wraps around the outside.

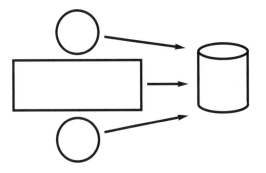

$$SA = 2 \text{ circles} + \text{rectangle} = 2(\pi r^2) + 2\pi rh$$

The only information you need to find the surface area of a cylinder is (1) the radius of the cylinder and (2) the height of the cylinder.

Cylinders and Volume

The volume of a cylinder measures how much "stuff" it can hold inside. In order to find the volume of a cylinder, use the following formula.

$$V = \pi r^2 h$$

V is the volume, *r* is the radius of the cylinder, and *h* is the height of the cylinder.

As with finding surface area, determining the volume of a cylinder requires two pieces of information: (1) the radius of the cylinder and (2) the height of the cylinder.

One way to remember this formula is to think of a cylinder as a stack of circles, each with an area or πr^2. Just multiply πr^2 × the height (h) of the shape to find the area.

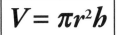

The diagram below shows that two cylinders can have the same volume but different shapes (and therefore each fits differently inside a larger object).

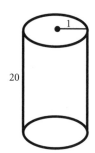

$$V = \pi r^2 h$$
$$= \pi(1)^2 20$$
$$= 20\pi$$

$$V = \pi r^2 h$$
$$= \pi(2)^2 5$$
$$= 20\pi$$

Check Your Skills Answers

1. **49π:** The formula for area is $A = \pi r^2$. The radius is 7, so Area = $\pi(7)^2 = 49\pi$.

2. **17:** Circumference of a circle is either $C = 2\pi r$ or $C = \pi d$. The question asks for the diameter, so we'll use the latter formula. $17\pi = \pi d$. Divide by π, and we get $17 = d$. The diameter is 17.

3. **10π:** The link between area and circumference of a circle is that they are both defined in terms of the radius. Area of a circle is $A = \pi r^2$, so we can use the area of the circle to find the radius. $25\pi = \pi r^2$, so $r = 5$. If the radius equals 5, then the circumference is $C = 2\pi(5)$, which equals 10π. The circumference is 10π.

4. **3π:** If the central angle of the sector is 270°, then it is 3/4 of the full circle, because $\dfrac{270°}{360°} = \dfrac{3}{4}$. If the radius is 2, then the area of the full circle is $\pi(2)^2$, which equals 4π. If the area of the full circle is 4π, then the area of the sector will be $3/4 \times 4\pi$, which equals 3π.

5. **240°:** To find the central angle, we first need to figure out what fraction of the circle the sector is. We can do that by finding the circumference of the full circle. The radius is 3, so the circumference of the circle is $2\pi(3) = 6\pi$. That means the sector is 2/3 of the circle, because $\dfrac{4\pi}{6\pi} = \dfrac{2}{3}$. That means the central angle of the sector is $2/3 \times 360°$, which equals 240°.

6. **8π:** We can begin by finding the area of the whole circle. The radius of the circle is 10, so the area is $\pi(10)^2$, which equals 100π. That means the sector is 2/5 of the circle, because $\dfrac{40\pi}{100\pi} = \dfrac{4}{10} = \dfrac{2}{5}$. We can find the circumference of the whole circle using $C = 2\pi r$. The circumference equals 20π. $2/5 \times 20\pi = 8\pi$. The arc length of the sector is 8π.

Problem Set (Note: Figures are not drawn to scale.)

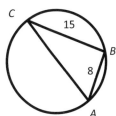

1. Triangle *ABC* is inscribed in a circle, such that *AC* is a diameter of the circle (see figure). If *AB* has a length of 8 and *BC* has a length of 15, what is the circumference of the circle?

2. A cylinder has a surface area of 360π, and is 3 units tall. What is the diameter of the cylinder's circular base?

3. Randy can run π meters every 2 seconds. If the circular track has a radius of 75 meters, how long does it take Randy to run twice around the track?

4. Randy then moves on to the Jumbo Track, which has a radius of 200 meters (as compared to the first track, with a radius of 75 meters). Ordinarily, Randy runs 8 laps on the normal track. How many laps on the Jumbo Track would Randy have to run in order to have the same workout?

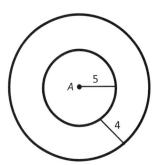

5. A circular lawn with a radius of 5 meters is surrounded by a circular walkway that is 4 meters wide (see figure). What is the area of the walkway?

6. A cylindrical water tank has a diameter of 14 meters and a height of 20 meters. A water truck can fill π cubic meters of the tank every minute. How long will it take the water truck to fill the water tank from empty to half-full?

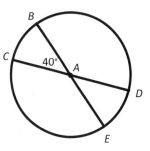

7. *BE* and *CD* are both diameters of Circle A (see figure). If the area of Circle A is 180 units^2, what is the area of sector *ABC* + sector *ADE*?

8. Jane has to paint a cylindrical column that is 14 feet high and that has a circular base with a radius of 3 feet. If one bucket of paint will cover 10π square feet, how many buckets does Jane need to buy in order to paint the column, including the top and bottom?

9. A circular flower bed takes up half the area of a square lawn. If an edge of the lawn is 200 feet long, what is the radius of the flower bed? (Express the answer in terms of π.)

10.   If angle *ABC* is 40 degrees (see figure), and the area of the circle is 81π, how long is arc *AXC*?

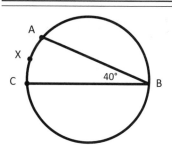

11.   Triangle *ABC* is inscribed in a circle, such that *AC* is a diameter of the circle and angle *BAC* is 45° (see figure). If the area of triangle *ABC* is 72 square units, how much larger is the area of the circle than the area of triangle *ABC*?

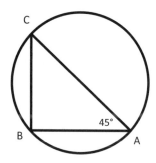

12.   Triangle *ABC* is inscribed in a circle, such that *AC* is a diameter of the circle and angle *BAC* is 45°. (Refer to the same figure as for problem #11.) If the area of triangle *ABC* is 84.5 square units, what is the length of arc *BC*?

13.

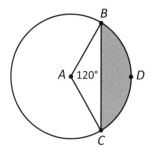

A is the center of the circle
above.

Column A	Column B
The perimeter of the shaded region	The perimeter of triangle ABC

14.

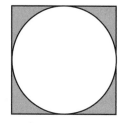

In the figure above, a circle
with area π is inscribed in a
square.

Column A	Column B
The combined area of the shaded regions	1

15.

Column A	Column B
The combined area of four circles, each with radius 1	The area of a circle with radius 2

1. **17π:** If AC is a diameter of the circle, then inscribed triangle ABC is a right triangle, with AC as the hypotenuse. Therefore, we can apply the Pythagorean Theorem to find the length of AC.

$$8^2 + 15^2 = c^2$$
$$64 + 225 = c^2 \qquad\qquad \text{The circumference of the circle is } 2\pi r, \text{ or } 17\pi.$$
$$c^2 = 289$$
$$c = 17 \qquad\qquad \text{You might recognize the common 8–15–17 right triangle.}$$

2. **24:** The surface area of a cylinder is the area of the circular top and bottom, plus the area of its wrapped-around rectangular third face. We can express this in formula form as:

$$SA = 2(\pi r^2) + 2\pi rh$$

Substitute the known values into this formula to find the radius of the circular base:

$$360\pi = 2(\pi r^2) + 2\pi r(3)$$
$$360\pi = 2\pi r^2 + 6\pi r$$
$$2\pi r^2 + 6\pi r - 360\pi = 0 \qquad\qquad \text{Divide by } 2\pi$$
$$r^2 + 3r - 180 = 0$$
$$(r + 15)(r - 12) = 0$$

$$r + 15 = 0 \qquad \text{OR} \qquad r - 12 = 0$$
$$r = \{-15, 12\}$$

Use only the positive value of r: 12. If $r = 12$, the diameter of the cylinder's circular base is 24.

3. **10 minutes:** The distance around the track is the circumference of the circle:

$$C = 2\pi r$$
$$= 150\pi$$

Running twice around the circle would equal a distance of 300π meters. If Randy can run π meters every 2 seconds, he runs 30π meters every minute. Therefore, it will take him 10 minutes to run around the circular track twice.

4. **3 laps:** 8 laps on the normal track is a distance of $1,200\pi$ meters. (Recall from problem #3 that the circumference of the normal track is 150π meters.) If the Jumbo Track has a radius of 200 meters, its circumference is 400π meters. It will take 3 laps around this track to travel $1,200\pi$ meters.

5. **$56\pi\text{m}^2$:** The area of the walkway is the area of the entire image (walkway + lawn) minus the area of the lawn. To find the area of each circle, use the formula:

Large circle: $A = \pi r^2 = \pi(9)^2 = 81\pi$
Small circle: $A = \pi r^2 = \pi(5)^2 = 25\pi$ $81\pi - 25\pi = 56\pi\text{m}^2$

6. **8 hours and 10 minutes:** First find the volume of the cylindrical tank:

$$V = \pi r^2 \times h$$
$$= \pi(7)^2 \times 20$$
$$= 980\pi$$

If the water truck can fill π cubic meters of the tank every minute, it will take 980 minutes to fill the tank completely; therefore, it will take $980 \div 2 = 490$ minutes to fill the tank halfway. This is equal to 8 hours and 10 minutes.

7. **40 units²:** The two central angles, *CAB* and *DAE*, describe a total of 80°. Simplify the fraction to find out what fraction of the circle this represents:

$$\frac{80}{360} = \frac{2}{9}$$ $\frac{2}{9}$ of 180 units² is 40 units².

8. **11 buckets:** The surface area of a cylinder is the area of the circular top and bottom, plus the area of its wrapped-around rectangular third face.

Top & Bottom: $A = \pi r^2 = 9\pi$
Rectangle: $A = 2\pi r \times h = 84\pi$

The total surface area, then, is $9\pi + 9\pi + 84\pi = 102\pi$ ft². If one bucket of paint will cover 10π ft², then Jane will need 10.2 buckets to paint the entire column. Since paint stores do not sell fractional buckets, she will need to purchase 11 buckets.

9. $\sqrt{\dfrac{20,000}{\pi}}$: The area of the lawn is $(200)^2 = 40,000$ ft².

Therefore, the area of the flower bed is $40,000 \div 2 = 20,000$ ft².

$A = \pi r^2 = 20,000$ The radius of the flower bed is equal to $\sqrt{\dfrac{20,000}{\pi}}$.

10. **4π :** If the area of the circle is 81π, then the radius of the circle is 9 ($A = \pi r^2$). Therefore, the total circumference of the circle is 18π ($C = 2\pi r$). Angle *ABC*, an inscribed angle of 40°, corresponds to a central angle of 80°. Thus, arc *AXC* is equal to 80/360 = 2/9 of the total circumference:

$2/9(18\pi) = 4\pi$.

11. **72π − 72:** If *AC* is a diameter of the circle, then angle *ABC* is a right angle. Therefore, triangle *ABC* is a 45–45–90 triangle, and the base and height are equal. Assign the variable *x* to represent both the base and height:

$A = \dfrac{bh}{2}$ $\dfrac{x^2}{2} = 72$

$x^2 = 144$
$x = 12$

The base and height of the triangle are equal to 12, and so the area of the triangle is $\dfrac{12 \times 12}{2} = 72$.

The hypotenuse of the triangle, which is also the diameter of the circle, is equal to $12\sqrt{2}$. Therefore, the radius is equal to $6\sqrt{2}$ and the area of the circle, πr^2, $= 72\pi$. The area of the circle is $72\pi - 72$ square units larger than the area of triangle *ABC*.

12. $\dfrac{13\sqrt{2}\pi}{4}$: We know that the area of triangle *ABC* is 84.5 square units, so we can use the same logic as in the previous problem to establish the base and height of the triangle:

$$A = \frac{bh}{2}$$

$$\frac{x^2}{2} = 84.5$$

$$x^2 = 169$$

$$x = 13$$

The base and height of the triangle are equal to 13. Therefore, the hypotenuse, which is also the diameter of the circle, is equal to $13\sqrt{2}$, and the circumference $(C = \pi d)$ is equal to $13\sqrt{2}\pi$. Angle A, an inscribed angle, corresponds to a central angle of 90°. Thus, arc $BC = 90/360 = 1/4$ of the total circumference:

$$\frac{1}{4} \text{ of } 13\sqrt{2}\pi \text{ is } \frac{13\sqrt{2}\pi}{4}.$$

13. **B:** Since the two perimeters share the line BC, we can recast this question as

Column A	Column B
The combined length of two radii (AB and AC)	The length of arc BDC

The easiest thing to do in this situation is use numbers. Assume the radius of the circle is 2.

If the radius is 2, then we can rewrite Column A.

Column A	Column B
The combined length of two radii (AB and AC) = 4	The length of arc BDC

Now we need to figure out the length of arc BDC if the radius is 2. We can set up a proportion, because the ratio of central angle to 360 will be the same as the ratio of the arc length to the circumference.

$$\frac{\text{Arc Length}}{\text{Circumference}} = \frac{120°}{360°} = \frac{1}{3}$$

Circumference is $2\pi r$, so

$$C = 2\pi(2) = 4?$$

Rewrite the proportion.

$$\frac{\text{Arc Length}}{4\pi} = \frac{1}{3}$$

$$\text{Arc Length} = \frac{4\pi}{3}$$

Rewrite Column B.

Column A	**Column B**
4	The length of arc $BDC = 4\pi/3$

Compare 4 to $4\pi/3$. π is greater than 3, so $4\pi/3$ is slightly greater than 4.

14. **B:** Use the area of the circle to determine the area of the square, then subtract the area of the circle from the area of the square to determine the shaded region. The formula for area is $A = \pi r^2$. If we substitute the area of this square for A, we can determine the radius:

$$\pi = \pi r^2$$
$$1 = r^2$$
$$1 = r$$

Since the radius of the circle is 1, the diameter of the circle is 2, as is each side of the square. A square with sides of 2 has an area of 4. Rewrite Column A.

Column A	**Column B**
The combined area of the shaded regions = $\text{Area}_{\text{Square}} - \text{Area}_{\text{Circle}} =$ **$4 - \pi$**	1

π is greater than 3, so $4 - \pi$ is less than 1.

15. **C:** First, evaluate Column A. Plug 1 in for r in the formula for the area of a circle:

$$A = \pi r^2$$
$$A = \pi(1)^2$$
$$A = \pi$$

Each circle has an area of π, and the four circles have a total area of 4π.

Column A	**Column B**
The combined area of four circles, each with radius 1 = **4π**	The area of a circle with radius 2

For Column B, plug 2 in for r in the formula for the area of a circle:

$$A = \pi r^2$$
$$A = \pi(2)^2$$
$$A = 4\pi$$

Column A	**Column B**
4π	The area of a circle with radius 2 = **4π**

g | Chapter 5
of

GEOMETRY

LINES &
ANGLES

In This Chapter . . .

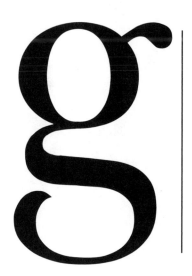

- Intersecting Lines
- Exterior Angles of a Triangle
- Parallel Lines Cut By a Transversal

LINES & ANGLES

A straight line is 180°. Think of a line as half of a circle.

Parallel lines are lines that lie in a plane and that never intersect. No matter how far you extend the lines, they never meet. Two parallel lines are shown below:

Perpendicular lines are lines that intersect at a 90° angle. Two perpendicular lines are shown below:

There are two major line-angle relationships that you must know for the GRE:
  (1) The angles formed by any intersecting lines.
  (2) The angles formed by parallel lines cut by a transversal.

Intersecting Lines

Intersecting lines have three important properties.

First, the interior angles formed by intersecting lines form a circle, so the sum of these angles is 360°. In the diagram shown, $a + b + c + d = 360$.

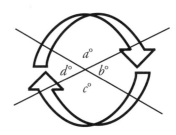

Second, interior angles that combine to form a line sum to 180°. These are termed **supplementary angles**. Thus, in the diagram shown, $a + b = 180$, because angles a and b form a line together. Other supplementary angles are $b + c = 180$, $c + d = 180$, and $d + a = 180$.

Third, angles found opposite each other where these two lines intersect are equal. These are called **vertical angles**. Thus, in the diagram above, $a = c$, because these angles are opposite one another, and are formed from the same two lines. Additionally, $b = d$ for the same reason.

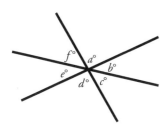

Note that these rules apply to more than two lines that intersect at a point, as shown to the left. In this diagram, $a + b + c + d + e + f = 360$, because these angles combine to form a circle. In addition, $a + b + c = 180$, because these three angles combine to form a line. Finally, $a = d$, $b = e$, and $c = f$, because they are pairs of vertical angles.

Check Your Skills

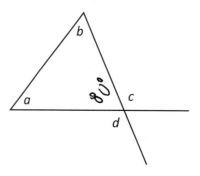

1. If $b + f = 150$, what is angle d? $30°$

2. What is $x - y$? 40

Answers can be found on page 105.

Exterior Angles of a Triangle

An **exterior angle** of a triangle is equal in measure to the sum of the two non-adjacent (opposite) **interior angles** of the triangle. For example:

$a + c$
EQUALS
x

$a + b + c = 180$ (sum of angles in a triangle).
$b + x = 180$ (supplementary angles).
Therefore, $x = a + c$.

This property is frequently tested on the GRE! In particular, look for exterior angles within more complicated diagrams. You might even redraw the diagram with certain lines removed to isolate the triangle and exterior angle you need.

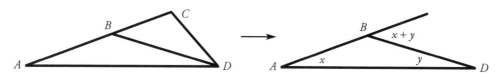

Check Your Skills

3. If $c + d = 200$, what is $a + b$? 100

Answers can be found on page 105.

Parallel Lines Cut By a Transversal

The GRE makes frequent use of diagrams that include parallel lines cut by a **transversal**.

Notice that there are 8 angles formed by this construction, but there are only TWO different angle measures (a and b). All the **acute** angles (less than 90°) in this diagram are equal. Likewise, all the **obtuse** angles (more than 90° but less than 180°) are equal. Any acute angle is supplementary to any obtuse angle. Thus, $a + b = 180°$.

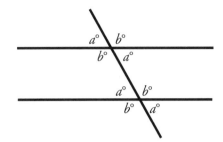

When you see a transversal cutting two lines that you know to be parallel, fill in all the a (acute) and b (obtuse) angles, just as in the diagram above.

Sometimes the GRE disguises the parallel lines and the transversal so that they are not readily apparent, as in the diagram pictured to the right.

In these disguised cases, it is a good idea to extend the lines so that you can easily see the parallel lines and the transversal. Just remember always to be on the lookout for parallel lines. When you see them, extend lines and label the acute and obtuse angles.

You might also mark the parallel lines with arrows.

Check Your Skills

Refer to the following diagram for questions 4–5.

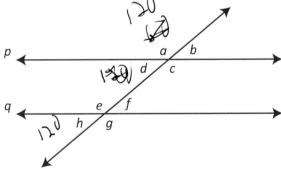
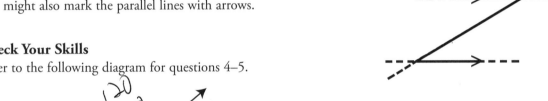

(lines p and q are parallel)

4. If angle $h = 120$, what is a?   60
5. If angle $h = 120$, what is $a + b + c$?   240

Answers can be found on page 105.

Check Your Skills Answers

1. **30:** Because they are vertical angles, angle a is equal to angle d.

Because they add to form a straight line, $a + b + f = 180$.
Substitute d for a to yield, $(d) + b + f = 180$. Substitute 150 for $b + f$ to yield $d + (150) = 180$. So $d = 180 - 150 = 30$.

2. **140:** Because x and 20 are supplementary, $x = 180 - 20 = 160$. Because y and 20 are vertical, $y = 20$. So $x - y = 160 - 20 = 140$.

3. **100:** Since c and d are vertical angles, they are equal. Since they sum to 200, each must be 100. $a + b = c$, because c is an exterior angle of the triangle shown, and a and b are the two non-adjacent interior angles. $a + b = c = 100$.

4. **120:** In a system of parallel lines cut by a transversal, opposite exterior angles (like a and h) are equal. $h = a = 120$.

5. **300:** From question 4, we know that $a = 120$. Since $a = 120$, its supplementary angle $d = 180 - 120 = 60$. Since $a + b + c + d = 360$, and $d = 60$, $a + b + c = 300$.

Problem Set

Problems 1–4 refer to the diagram on the right, where line *AB* is parallel to line *CD*.

1.   If $x - y = 10$, what is *x*?

2.   If the ratio of *x* to *y* is 3 : 2, what is *y*?

3.   If $x + (x + y) = 320$, what is *x*?

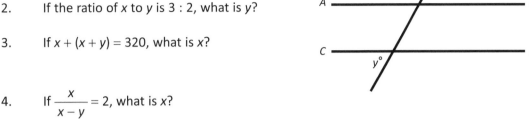

4.   If $\dfrac{x}{x - y} = 2$, what is *x*?

Problems 5–8 refer to the diagram on the right.

5.   If *a* is 95, what is $b + d - e$?

6.   If $c + f = 70$, and $d = 80$, what is *b*?

7.   If *a* and *b* are **complementary angles** (they sum
      to 90°), name three other pairs of
      complementary angles.

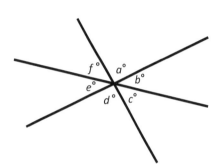

8.   If *e* is 45, what is the sum of all the other angles?

Problems 9–12 refer to the diagram on the right, where line *XY* is parallel to line *QU*.

9.   If $a + e = 150$, find *f*.

10.   If $a = y$, $g = 3y + 20$, and $f = 2x$, find *x*.

11.   If $g = 11y$, $a = 4x - y$, and $d = 5y + 2x - 20$,
      find *h*.

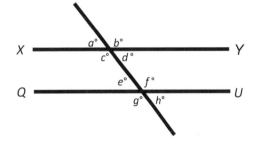

12.   If $b = 4x$, $e = x + 2y$, and $d = 3y + 8$, find *h*.

Problems 13–15 refer to the diagram to the right.

13.   If $c + g = 140$, find *k*.

14.   If $g = 90$, what is $a + k$?

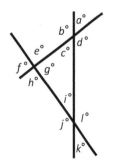

15.   If $f + k = 150$, find *b*.

16.

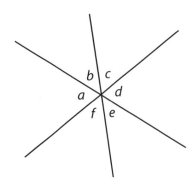

Column A

$a + f + b$

Column B

$c + d + e$

17.

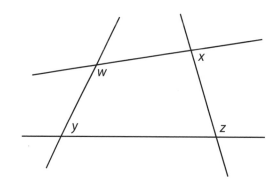

Column A

$w + y$

Column B

$x + z$

18.

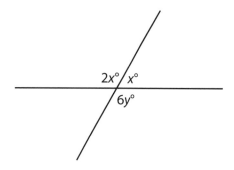

Column A

y

Column B

10

1. **95:** We know that $x + y = 180$, since any acute angle formed by a transversal that cuts across two parallel lines is supplementary to any obtuse angle. Use the information given to set up a system of two equations with two variables:

$$\begin{aligned} x + y &= 180 \\ \underline{x - y} &= \underline{10} \\ 2x &= 190 \\ x &= 95 \end{aligned}$$

2. **72:** Set up a ratio, using the unknown multiplier, a.

$$\frac{x}{y} = \frac{3a}{2a}$$

$$180 = x + y = 3a + 2a = 5a$$
$$180 = 5a$$
$$a = 36$$
$$y = 2a = 2(36) = 72$$

3. **140:** Use the fact that $x + y = 180$ to set up a system of two equations with two variables:

$$\begin{aligned} x + y = 180 \quad &\rightarrow \quad -x - y = -180 \\ &+ \quad \underline{2x + y = 320} \\ & x = 140 \end{aligned}$$

4. **120:** Use the fact that $x + y = 180$ to set up a system of two equations with two variables:

$$\begin{aligned} \frac{x}{x - y} = 2 \quad &\rightarrow \quad x - 2y = 0 \\ &- \quad \underline{x + y = 180} \\ & -3y = -180 \\ & y = 60 \quad \rightarrow \quad \text{Therefore, } x = 120. \end{aligned}$$

5. **95:** Because a and d are vertical angles, they have the same measure: $a = d = 95°$. Likewise, since b and e are vertical angles, they have the same measure: $b = e$. Therefore, $b + d - e = d = 95°$.

6. **65:** Because c and f are vertical angles, they have the same measure: $c + f = 70$, so $c = f = 35$. Notice that b, c, and d form a straight line: $b + c + d = 180$. Substitute the known values of c and d into this equation:

$$\begin{aligned} b + 35 + 80 &= 180 \\ b + 115 &= 180 \\ b &= 65 \end{aligned}$$

7. **b and d, a and e, & d and e:** If a is complementary to b, then d (which is equal to a, since they are vertical angles), is also complementary to b. Likewise, if a is complementary to b, then a is also complementary to e (which is equal to b, since they are vertical angles). Finally, d and e must be complementary, since $d = a$ and $e = b$. You do not need to know the term "complementary," but you should be able to work with the concept (two angles adding up to 90°).

8. **315:** If $e = 45$, then the sum of all the other angles is $360 - 45 = 315°$.

9. **105:** We are told that $a + e = 150$. Since they are both acute angles formed by a transversal cutting across two parallel lines, they are also congruent. Therefore, $a = e = 75$. Any acute angle in this diagram is supplementary to any obtuse angle, so $75 + f = 180$, and $f = 105$.

10. **70:** We know that angles a and g are supplementary; their measures sum to 180. Therefore:

$$y + 3y + 20 = 180$$
$$4y = 160$$
$$y = 40$$

Angle f is congruent to angle g, so its measure is also $3y + 20$. The measure of angle $f = g = 3(40) + 20 = 140$. If $f = 2x$, then $140 = 2x \rightarrow x = 70$.

11. **70:** We are given the measure of one acute angle (a) and one obtuse angle (g). Since any acute angle in this diagram is supplementary to any obtuse angle, $11y + 4x - y = 180$, or $4x + 10y = 180$. Since angle d is congruent to angle a, we know that $5y + 2x - 20 = 4x - y$, or $2x - 6y = -20$. We can set up a system of two equations with two variables:

$$2x - 6y = -20 \quad \rightarrow$$

$$\begin{array}{r} -4x + 12y = 40 \\ 4x + 10y = 180 \\ \hline 22y = 220 \\ y = 10; \ x = 20 \end{array}$$

Since h is one of the acute angles, h has the same measure as a: $4x - y = 4(20) - 10 = 70$.

12. **68:** Because b and d are supplementary, $4x + 3y + 8 = 180$, or $4x + 3y = 172$. Since d and e are congruent, $3y + 8 = x + 2y$, or $x - y = 8$. We can set up a system of two equations with two variables:

$$x - y = 8 \qquad \rightarrow \qquad \begin{array}{r} 4x + 3y = 172 \\ 3x - 3y = 24 \\ \hline 7x = 196 \\ x = 28; \ y = 20 \end{array}$$

Since h is congruent to d, $h = 3y + 8$, or $3(20) + 8 = 68$.

13. **40:** If $c + g = 140$, then $i = 40$, because there are 180° in a triangle. Since k is vertical to i, k is also = 40. Alternately, if $c + g = 140$, then $j = 140$, since j is an exterior angle of the triangle and is therefore equal to the sum of the two remote interior angles. Since k is supplementary to j, $k = 180 - 140 = 40$.

14. **90:** If $g = 90$, then the other two angles in the triangle, c and i, sum to 90. Since a and k are vertical angles to c and i, they sum to 90 as well.

15. **150:** Angles f and k are vertical to angles g and i. These two angles, then, must also sum to 150. Angle b, an exterior angle of the triangle, must be equal to the sum of the two remote interior angles g and i. Therefore, $b = 150$.

16. **C:** You can substitute each of the values in Column A for a corresponding value in Column B. $a = d$, $c = f$, and $b = e$, in each case because the equal angles are vertical angles. Rewrite Column A.

Column A	**Column B**
$a + f + b = (d) + (c) + (e)$	$c + d + e$

17. **C:** To see why the sums in the two columns are equal, label the remaining two interior angles of the quadrilateral a and b.

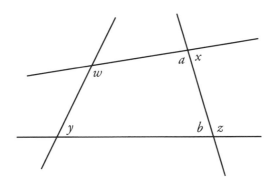

Column A	**Column B**
$w + y$	$x + z$

There are several relationships we can describe based on the diagram. For instance, we know the sum of the four internal angles of the quadrilateral is 360.

$$w + y + a + b = 360$$

We also have two pairs of supplementary angles.

$$a + x = 180$$
$$b + z = 180$$

Add the two equations together:

$$a + b + x + z = 360$$

$w + y + a + b$ sum to 360, as do $a + b + x + z$. Therefore the two sums equal each other.

$$w + y + a + b = a + b + x + z \qquad \text{Subtract } a + b \text{ from both sides}$$
$$w + y = x + z$$

The two columns are equal.

18. **A:** First solve for x. The two angles x and $2x$ are supplementary.

$$x + 2x = 180$$
$$3x = 180$$
$$x = 60$$

Next note that $2x = 6y$, because $2x$ and $6y$ are vertical angles. Plug in 60 for x and solve for y.

$$2(60) = 6y$$
$$120 = 6y$$
$$20 = y$$

<u>Column A</u>

$y = 20$

<u>Column B</u>

10

Chapter 6
of
GEOMETRY

THE COORDINATE
PLANE

In This Chapter . . .

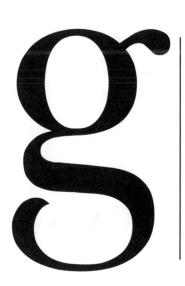

The Number Line—Redux

Before we discuss the coordinate plane, let's review the number line.

The Number Line

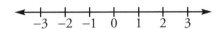

The number line is a ruler or measuring stick that goes as far as we want in both directions. With the number line, we can say where something is with a single number. In other words, we can link a position with a number.

Position	Number	Number Line
"Two units right of zero"	2	
"One and a half units left of zero"	−1.5	

We use both positive and negative numbers, because we want to indicate positions both left and right of zero.

You might be wondering "The position of what?" The answer is, a **point**, which is just a dot. When we are dealing with the number line, a point and a number mean the same thing.

If you show me where the point is on the number line, I can tell you the number.   → *the point is at −2*

If you tell me the number, I can show you where the point is on the number line.   *the point is at 0* →

This works even if we only have partial information about our point. If you tell me *something* about where the point is, I can tell you *something* about the number, and vice-versa.

For instance, if I say that the number is positive, then I know that the point lies somewhere to the right of 0 on the number line. Even though I don't know the exact location of the point, I do know a range of potential values.

The number is positive.
In other words, the number is greater than (>) 0.

This also works in reverse. If I see a range of potential positions on a number line, I can tell you what that range is for the number.

 The number is less than (<) 0.

Everything we've done so far should be familiar. We discussed the number line and inequalities in the last chapter. But now let's make things more complicated. What if we want to be able to locate a point that's not on a straight line, but on a page?

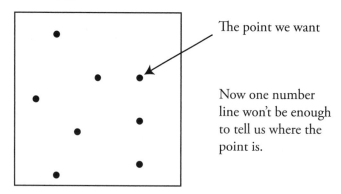

The point we want

Now one number line won't be enough to tell us where the point is.

Let's begin by inserting our number line into the picture. This will help us determine how far to the right or left of 0 our point is.

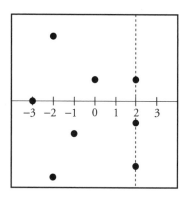

The point is two units to the right of zero.

But all three points that touch the dotted line are two units to the right of zero. We don't have enough information to determine the unique location of our point.

In order to know the location of our point, we also need to know how far up or down the dotted line we need to go. To determine how far up or down we need to go, we're going to need another number line. This number line, however, is going to be vertical. Using this vertical number line, we will be able to measure how far above or below 0 a point is.

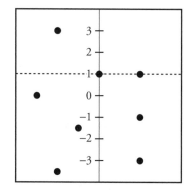

The point is one unit above zero.

Notice that this number line by itself also does not provide enough information to determine the unique location of the point.

But, if we combine the information from the two number lines, we can determine both how far left or right *and* how far up or down the point is.

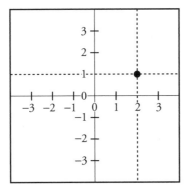

The point is 2 units to the right of 0.

AND

The point is 1 unit above 0.

Now we have a unique description of the point's position. There is only one point on the page that is BOTH 2 units to the right of 0 AND 1 unit above 0. So, on a page, we need two numbers to indicate position.

Just as with the number line, information can travel in either direction. If we know the two numbers that give the location, we can place that point on the page.

The point is 3 units to the left of 0.

AND

The point is 2 unit below 0.

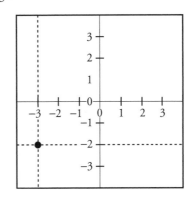

If, on the other hand, we see a point on the page, we can identify its location and determine the two numbers.

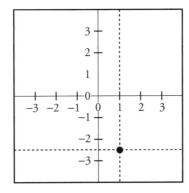

The point is 1 units to the right of 0.

AND

The point is 2.5 units below 0.

Now that we have two pieces of information for each point, we need to keep straight which number is which. In other words, we need to know which number gives the left-right position and which number gives the up-down position.

To represent the difference, we use some technical terms:

The ***x*-coordinate** is the left right-number.

    Numbers to the right of 0 are positive.
    Numbers to the left of 0 are negative.

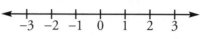

This number line is the ***x*-axis.**

The ***y*-coordinate** is the up-down number.

    Numbers above 0 are positive.
    Numbers below 0 are negative.

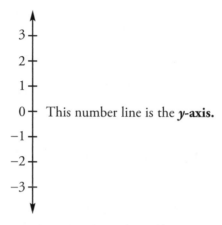

This number line is the ***y*-axis.**

Now, when describing the location of a point, we can use the technical terms.

The *x*-coordinate of the point is 1 and
the *y*-coordinate of the point is 0.

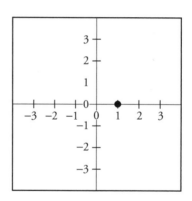

We can condense this and say that, for this point, $x = 1$ and $y = 0$. In fact, we can go even further. We can say that the point is at (1, 0). This shorthand always has the same basic layout. The first number in the parentheses is the *x*-coordinate, and the second number is the *y*-coordinate. One easy way to remember this is that *x* comes before *y* in the alphabet.

The point is at (−3, −1)

OR

The point has an *x*-coordinate
of −3 and a *y*-coordinate of −1.

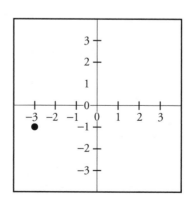

Now we have a fully functioning **coordinate plane:** an *x*-axis and a *y*-axis drawn on a page. The coordinate plane allows us to determine the unique position of any point on a **plane** (essentially, a really big and flat sheet of paper).

And in case you were ever curious about what **one-dimensional** and **two-dimensional** mean, now you know. A line is one dimensional, because you only need *one* number to identify a point's location. A plane is two-dimensional because you need *two* numbers to identify a point's location.

Check Your Skills

1. Draw a coordinate plane and plot the following points:

      1. (3, 1)   2. (−2, 3.5)   3. (0, −4.5)   4. (1, 0)

2. Which point on the coordinate plane below is indicated by the following coordinates?

      1. (2, -1)   2. (−1.5, −3)   3. (−1, 2)   4. (3, 2)

Answers can be found on page 137.

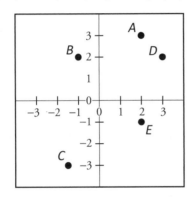

Knowing Just One Coordinate

As we've just seen, we need to know both the *x*-coordinate and the *y*-coordinate to plot a point exactly on the coordinate plane. If we only know one coordinate, we can't tell precisely where the point is, but we can narrow down the possibilities.

Consider this situation. Let's say that this is all we know: the point is 4 units to the right of 0.

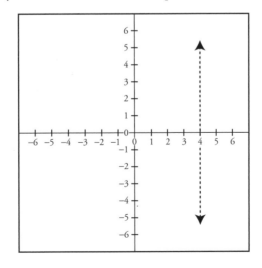

As we saw earlier, any point along the vertical dotted line is 4 units to the right of 0. In other words, every point on the dotted line has an *x*-coordinate of 4. We could shorten that and say $x = 4$. We don't know anything about the *y*-coordinate, which could be any number. All the points along the dotted line have different *y*-coordinates but the same *x*-coordinate, which equals 4.

So, if we know that $x = 4$, then our point can be anywhere along a vertical line that crosses the *x*-axis at (4, 0). Let's try with another example.

If we know that $x = -3$...

Then we know

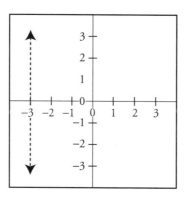

Every point on the dotted line has an *x*-coordinate of −3.

Points on the dotted line include (−3, 1), (−3, −7), (−3, 100) and so on. In general, if we know the *x*-coordinate of a point and not the *y*-coordinate, then all we can say about the point is that it lies on a vertical line.

The *x*-coordinate still indicates left-right position. If we fix that position but not the up-down position, then the point can only move up and down—forming a vertical line.

Now imagine that all we know is the *y*-coordinate of a number. Let's say we know that $y = -2$. How could we represent this on the coordinate plane? In other words, what are all the points for which $y = -2$?

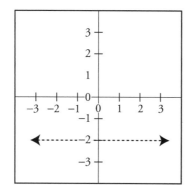

Every point 2 units below 0 fits this condition. These points form a horizontal line. We don't know anything about the *x*-coordinate, which could be any number. All the points along the horizontal dotted line have different *x*-coordinates but the same *y*-coordinate, which equals −2. For instance, (−3, −2), (−2, −2), (50, −2) are all on the line.

Let's try another example. If we know that $y = 1$...

Then we know

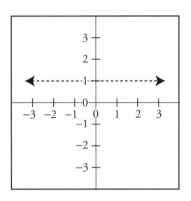

Every point on the dotted line has an y-coordinate of 1.

If we know the y-coordinate but not the x-coordinate, then we know the point lies somewhere on a horizontal line.

Check Your Skills

Draw a coordinate plane and plot the following lines.

3. $x = 6$
4. $y = -2$
5. $x = 0$

Answers can be found on pages 137–138.

Knowing Ranges

Now let's provide even less information. Instead of knowing the actual x-coordinate, let's see what happens if all we know is a range of possible values for x. What do we do if all we know is that $x > 0$? To answer that, let's return to the number line for a moment. As we saw earlier, if $x > 0$, then the target is anywhere to the right of 0.

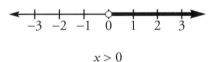

$x > 0$

Now let's look at the coordinate plane. All we know is that x is greater than 0. And we don't know *anything* about y, which could be any number.

How do we show all the possible points? We can shade in part of the coordinate plane: the part to the right of 0.

If we know that $x > 0$…

Then we know

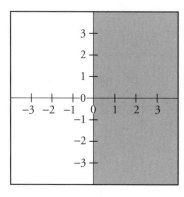

Every point in the shaded region has an x-coordinate greater than 0.

Now let's say that all we know is $y < 0$. Then we can shade in the bottom half of the coordinate plane—where the y-coordinate is less than 0. The x-coordinate can be anything.

If we know that $y < 0$…

Then we know

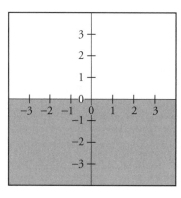

Every point in the shaded region has a y-coordinate less than 0.

Finally, if we know information about both x and y, then we can narrow down the shaded region.

If we know that $x > 0$ AND $y < 0$…

Then we know

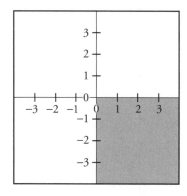

The only place where x is greater than 0 AND y is less than 0 is the bottom right quarter of the plane. So we know that the point lies somewhere in the bottom right quarter of the coordinate plane.

The four quarters of the coordinate plane are called **quadrants.** Each quadrant corresponds to a different combination of signs of x and y. The quadrants are always numbered as shown below, starting on the top right and going counter-clockwise.

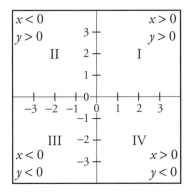

Check Your Skills

6. Which quadrant do the following points lie in?
     1. $(1, -2)$ 2. $(-4.6, 7)$ 3. $(-1, -2.5)$ 4. $(3, 3)$

7. Which quadrant or quadrants are indicated by the following?
     1. $x < 0, y > 0$ 2. $x < 0, y < 0$ 3. $y > 0$ 4. $x < 0$

Answers can be found on page 138.

Reading a Graph

If we see a point on a coordinate plane, we can read off its coordinates as follows. To find an x-coordinate, drop an imaginary line down to the x-axis (if the point is above the x-axis) or draw a line up to the x-axis (if the point is below the x-axis) and read off the number.

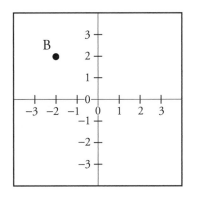 $\longrightarrow$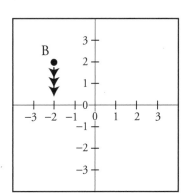

The line hit the *x*-axis at −2, which means the *x*-coordinate of our point is −2. Now, to find the *y*-coordinate, we employ a similar technique, only now we draw a horizontal line instead of a vertical line.

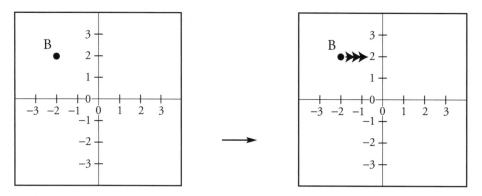

Our line touched the *y*-axis at 2, which means the *y*-coordinate of our point is 2. Thus, the coordinates of point B are (−2, 2).

Now suppose that we know the target is on a slanted line in the plane. We can read coordinates off of this slanted line. Try this problem on your own first.

> On the line shown, what is the *y* coordinate of the point that has an *x*-coordinate of −4?

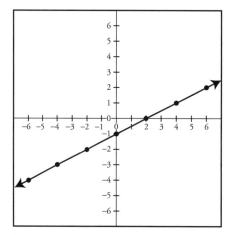

To answer this question, think about reading the coordinates of a point. We went from the point to the axes. Here, we will go from the axis that we know (here, the *x*-axis) to the line that contains the point, and then to the *y*-axis (the axis we don't know).

*Manhattan*GRE*Prep
the new standard

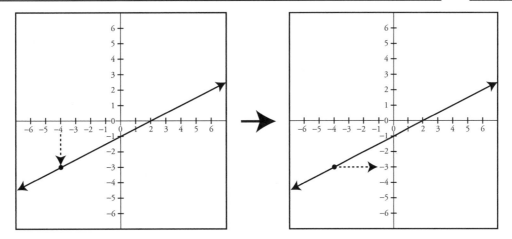

So the point on the line that has an *x*-coordinate of −4 has a *y*-coordinate of −3.

This method of locating points applies equally well to any shape or curve you may encounter on a coordinate plane. Try this next problem.

On the curve shown, what is the value of *y* when *x* = 2?

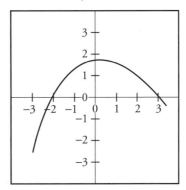

Once again, we know the *x*-coordinate, so we draw a line from the *x*-axis (where we know the coordinate) to the curve, and then draw a line to the *y*-axis.

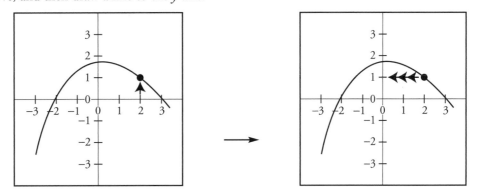

On the curve shown, the point that has an *x*-coordinate of 2 has a *y*-coordinate of 1.

Note that the GRE will mathematically define each line or curve, so you will never be forced to guess visually where a point falls. This discussion is meant to convey how to use any graphical representation.

Check Your Skills

8. On the following graph, what is the y-coordinate of the point on the line that has an x-coordinate of −3?

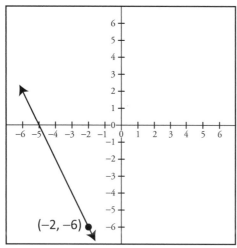

(−2, −6)

The answer can be found on page 138.

Plotting a Relationship

The most frequent use of the coordinate plane is to display a relationship between x and y. Often, this relationship is expressed this way: if you tell me x, I can tell you y.

As an equation, this sort of relationship looks like this:

y = some expression involving x Another way of saying this is we have y "in terms of" x

Examples: $y = 2x + 1$ If you plug a number in for x in any of these
             $y = x^2 − 3x + 2$ equations, you can calculate a value for y.

$$y = \frac{x}{x+2}$$

Let's take $y = 2x + 1$. We can generate a set of y's by plugging in various values of x. Start by making a table.

x	$y = 2x + 1$
−1	$y = 2(−1) + 1 = −1$
0	$y = 2(0) + 1 = 1$
1	$y = 2(1) + 1 = 3$
2	$y = 2(2) + 1 = 5$

Now that we have some values, let's see what we can do with them. We can say that when x equals 0, y equals 1. These two values form a pair. We express this connection by plotting the point (0, 1) on the coordinate plane. Similarly, we can plot all the other points that represent an x-y pair from our table:

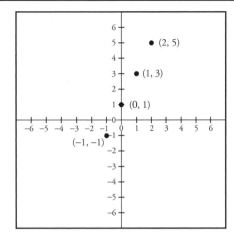

You might notice that these points seem to lie on a straight line. You're right—they do. In fact, any point that we can generate using the relationship $y = 2x + 1$ will also lie on the line.

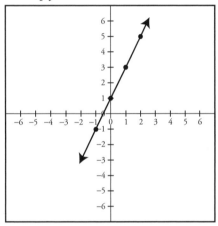

This line is the graphical representation of $y = 2x + 1$

So now we can talk about equations in visual terms. In fact, that's what lines and curves on the coordinate plane are—they represent all the *x-y* pairs that make an equation true. Take a look at the following example:

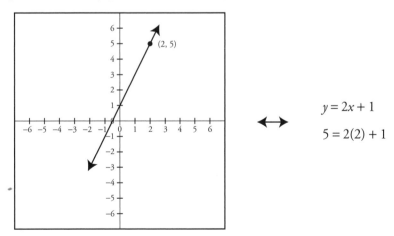

$$y = 2x + 1$$
$$5 = 2(2) + 1$$

The point (2, 5) lies on the line $y = 2x + 1$ ⟷   If we plug in 2 for x in $y = 2x + 1$, we get 5 for y

We can even speak more generally, using variables.

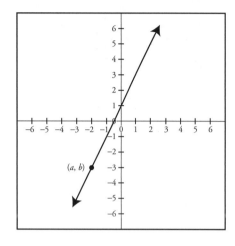   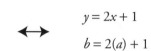

$$y = 2x + 1$$
$$b = 2(a) + 1$$

The point (a, b) lies on the line $y = 2x + 1$ ⟷   If we plug in a for x in $y = 2x + 1$, we get b for y

Check Your Skills

9. True or False? The point (9, 21) is on the line $y = 2x + 1$
10. True or False? The point (4, 14) is on the curve $y = x^2 - 2$

Answers can be found on page 138.

Lines in the Plane

The relationship $y = 2x + 1$ formed a line in the coordinate plane, as we saw. We can actually generalize this relationship. *Any* relationship of the following form represents a line:

$y = mx + b$ m and b represent numbers (positive or negative)

For instance, in the equation $y = 2x + 1$, we can see that m = 2 and b = 1.

Lines		Not Lines
$y = 3x - 2$	$m = 3, b = -2$	$y = x^2$
$y = -x + 4$	$m = -1, b = 4$	$y = \dfrac{1}{x}$
These are called linear equations.		These equations are not linear.

The numbers m and b have special meanings when we are dealing with linear equations. $m = $ **slope.** This tells us how steep the line is and whether the line is rising or falling.

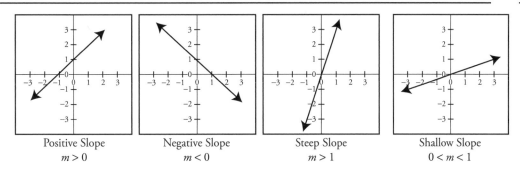

Positive Slope
$m > 0$

Negative Slope
$m < 0$

Steep Slope
$m > 1$

Shallow Slope
$0 < m < 1$

b = **y-intercept.** This tells you where the line crosses the y-axis. Any line or curve crosses the y-axis when $x = 0$. To find the y-intercept, plus in 0 for x into the equation.

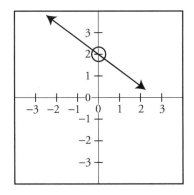

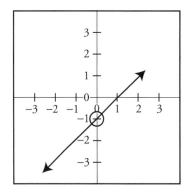

By recognizing linear equations and identifying m and b, we can plot a line more quickly than by plotting several points on the line.

Check Your Skills

What are the slope and y-intercept of the following lines?

11. $y = 3x + 4$
12. $2y = 5x - 12$

$2.5 - 6$

Answers can be found on page 139.

Now the question becomes, how do we use m and b to sketch a line? Let's plot the line $y = \frac{1}{2}x - 2$.

The easiest way to begin graphing a line is to begin with the y-intercept. We know that the line crosses the y-axis at $y = -2$, so let's begin by plotting that point on our coordinate plane.

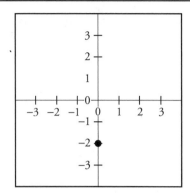

Now we need to figure out how to use slope in order to finish drawing our line. Every slope, whether an integer or a fraction, should be thought of as a fraction. In this equation, our m is 1/2. Let's look at the parts of the fraction and see what they can tell us about our slope.

$$\frac{1}{2} \;\rightarrow\; \frac{\text{Numerator}}{\text{Denominator}} \;\rightarrow\; \frac{\text{Rise}}{\text{Run}} \;\rightarrow\; \frac{\text{Change in } y}{\text{Change in } x}$$

The numerator of our fraction tells us how many units we want to move in the y direction—in other words, how far up or down we want to move. The denominator tells us how many units we want to move in the x direction—in other words, how far left or right we want to move. For this particular equation, the slope is 1/2, which means we want to move up 1 unit and right 2 units.

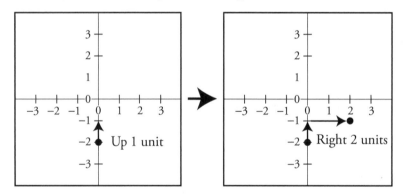

After we went up 1 unit and right 2 units, we ended up at the point (2, −1). What that means is that the point (2, −1) is also a solution to the equation $y = \frac{1}{2}x - 2$. In fact, we can plug in the x value and solve for y to check that we did this correctly.

$$y = \tfrac{1}{2}x - 2 \;\rightarrow\; y = \tfrac{1}{2}(2) - 2 \;\rightarrow\; y = 1 - 2 \;\rightarrow\; y = -1$$

What this means is that we can use the slope to generate points and draw our line. If we go up another 1 unit and right another 2 units, we will end up with another point that appears on the line. Although we could keep doing this indefinitely, in reality, with only 2 points we can figure out what our line looks like. Now all we need to do is draw the line that connects the 2 points we have, and we're done.

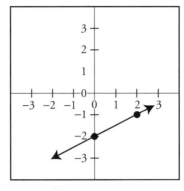

$y = \frac{1}{2}x - 2$

That means that this line is the graphical representation of $y = \frac{1}{2}x - 2$.

Let's try another one. Graph the equation $y = (\frac{-3}{2})x + 4$.

Once again, the best way to start is to plot the y-intercept. In this equation, $b = 4$, so we know the line crosses the y-axis at the point $(0, 4)$

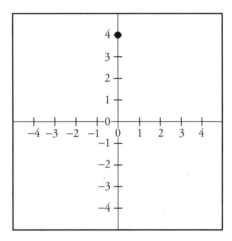

Now we can use the slope to find a second point. This time, the slope is $-3/2$, which is a negative slope. While positive slopes go up and to the right, negative slopes go down and to the right. Now, to find the next point, we need to go *down* 3 units and right 2 units.

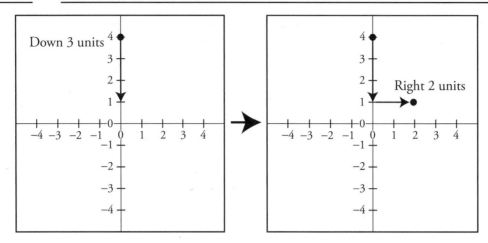

That means that (2, 1) is another point on the line. Now that we have 2 points, we can draw our line.

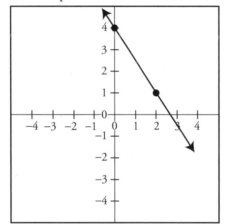

$$y = (^{-3}/_2)x + 4$$

Check Your Skills

13. Draw a coordinate plane and graph the line $y = 2x - 4$. Identify the slope and the *y*-intercept.

The answer can be found on page 139.

The Intercepts of a Line

A point where a line intersects a coordinate axis is called an **intercept**. There are two types of intercepts: the *x*-intercept, where the line intersects the *x*-axis, and the *y*-intercept, where the line intersects the *y*-axis.

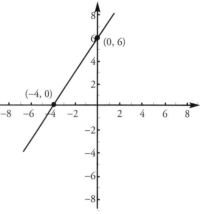

The x-intercept is expressed using the ordered pair $(x, 0)$, where x is the point where the line intersects the x-axis. **The x-intercept is the point on the line at which $y = 0$.** In this diagram, the x-intercept is -4, as expressed by the ordered pair $(-4, 0)$.

The y-intercept is expressed using the ordered pair $(0, y)$, where y is the point where the line intersects the y-axis. **The y-intercept is the point on the line at which $x = 0$.** In this diagram, the y-intercept is 6, as expressed by the ordered pair $(0, 6)$.

To find x-intercepts, <u>plug in 0 for y</u>. To find y-intercepts, <u>plug in 0 for x</u>.

The Intersection of Two Lines

Recall that a line in the coordinate plane is defined by a linear equation relating x and y. That is, if a point (x, y) lies on the line, then those values of x and y satisfy the equation. For instance, the point $(3, 2)$ lies on the line defined by the equation $y = 4x - 10$, since the equation is true when we plug in $x = 3$ and $y = 2$:

$$y = 4x - 10$$
$$2 = 4(3) - 10 = 12 - 10$$
$$2 = 2 \quad \text{TRUE}$$

On the other hand, the point $(7, 5)$ does not lie on that line, because the equation is false when we plug in $x = 7$ and $y = 5$:

$$y = 4x - 10$$
$$5 = 4(7) - 10 = 28 - 10 = 18? \quad \text{FALSE}$$

So, what does it mean when two lines intersect in the coordinate plane? It means that at the point of intersection, BOTH equations representing the lines are true. That is, the pair of numbers (x, y) that represents the point of intersection solves BOTH equations. Finding this point of intersection is equivalent to solving a system of two linear equations. You can find the intersection by using algebra more easily than by graphing the two lines.

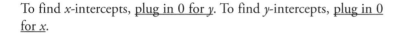

At what point does the line represented by $y = 4x - 10$ intersect the line represented by $2x + 3y = 26$?

Since $y = 4x - 10$, replace y in the second equation with $4x - 10$ and solve for x:

$$2x + 3(4x - 10) = 26$$
$$2x + 12x - 30 = 26$$
$$14x = 56$$
$$x = 4$$

Now solve for y. You can use either equation, but the first one is more convenient:

$y = 4x - 10$
$y = 4(4) - 10$
$y = 16 - 10 = 6$

Thus, the point of intersection of the two lines is (4, 6).

If two lines in a plane do not intersect, then the lines are parallel. If this is the case, there is NO pair of numbers (x, y) that satisfies both equations at the same time.

Two linear equations can represent two lines that intersect at a single point, or they can represent parallel lines that never intersect. There is one other possibility: the two equations might represent the same line. In this case, infinitely many points (x, y) along the line satisfy the two equations (which must actually be the same equation in two disguises).

Check Your Skills

14. What are the x- and y-intercepts of the equation $x - 2y = 8$?

Answers can be found on page 139.

The Distance Between 2 Points

The distance between any two points in the coordinate plane can be calculated by using the Pythagorean Theorem. For example:

What is the distance between the points (1, 3) and (7, −5)?

(1) Draw a right triangle connecting the points.

(2) Find the lengths of the two legs of the triangle by calculating the rise and the run.

The y-coordinate changes from 3 to −5, a difference of 8 (the vertical leg).

The x-coordinate changes from 1 to 7, a difference of 6 (the horizontal leg).

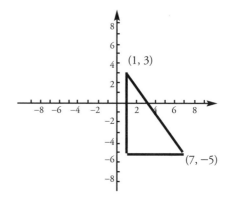

(3) Use the Pythagorean Theorem to calculate the length of the diagonal, which is the distance between the points.

$6^2 + 8^2 = c^2$
$36 + 64 = c^2$
$100 = c^2$
$c = 10$

The distance between the two points is 10 units.

Alternatively, to find the hypotenuse, we might have recognized this triangle as a variation of a 3–4–5 triangle (specifically, a 6–8–10 triangle).

Check Your Skills

15. What is the distance between (−2, −4) and (3, 8)?

Answers can be found on page 140.

Check Your Skills Answers

1.

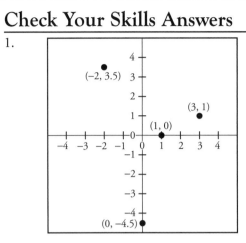

2.   1. (2, −1): **E**
       2. (−1.5, −3): **C**
       3. (−1, 2): **B**
       4. (3, 2): **D**

3.

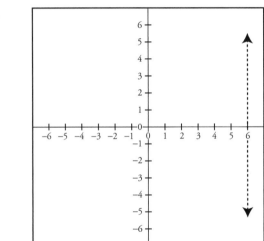

$x = 6$

4.

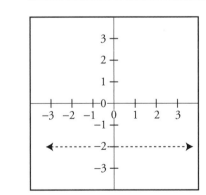

$y = -2$

5.

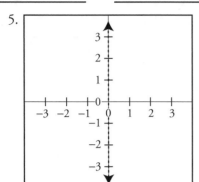

$x = 0$ is the y-axis.

6.   1. $(1, -2)$ is in Quadrant IV
      2. $(-4.6, 7)$ is in Quadrant II
      3. $(-1, -2.5)$ is in Quadrant III
      4. $(3, 3)$ is in Quadrant I

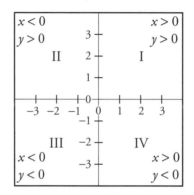

7.   1. $x < 0$, $y > 0$ indicates Quadrant II
      2. $x < 0$, $y < 0$ indicates Quadrant III
      3. $y > 0$ indicates Quadrants I and II
      4. $x < 0$ indicates Quadrants II and III

8. The point on the line with $x = -3$
   has a y-coordinate of -4.

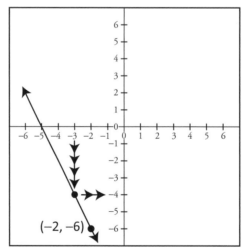

9. **False.** The relationship is $y = 2x + 1$, and the point we are testing is $(9, 21)$. So we plug in 9 for x and see if we get 21 for y. $y = 2(9) + 1 = 19$. The point $(9, 21)$ does not lie on the line.

10. **True.** The relationship is $y = x^2 - 2$, and the point we are testing is $(4, 14)$. So we plug in 4 for x and see if we get 14 for y. $y = (4)2 - 2 = 14$. The point $(4, 14)$ lies on the curve.

11. **Slope is 4, y-intercept is 4.** The equation $y = 3x + 4$ is already in $y = mx + b$ form, so we can directly find the slope and y-intercept. The slope is 3, and the y-intercept is 4.

12. **Slope is 2.5, y-intercept is −6.** To find the slope and y-intercept of a line, we need the equation to be in $y = mx + b$ form. We need to divide our original equation by 2 to make that happen. So $2y = 5x − 12$ becomes $y = 2.5x − 6$. So the slope is 2.5 (or 5/2) and the y-intercept is −6.

13.

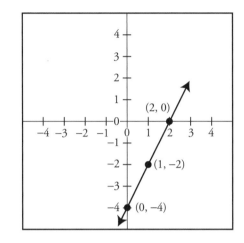

$y = 2x − 4$

slope $= 2$

y-intercept $= −4$

14. **x-intercept is 8, y-intercept is −4:**

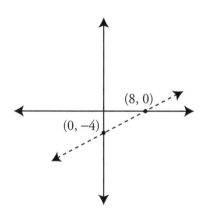

We've illustrated the line on the coordinate plane above, but you can also answer this question using algebra.

To determine the x-intercept, set y equal to 0, then solve for x:

$x − 2y = 8$
$y = 0$
$x − 0 = 8$
$x = 8$

To determine the y-intercept, set x equal to 0, then solve for y:

$x − 2y = 8$
$x = 0$
$0 − 2y = 8$
$−2y = 8$
$y = −4$

15. **13:** Answer: 13

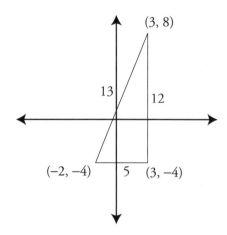

Explanation: The illustration above shows the two points. We have constructed a right triangle by finding a point directly below (3, 8) and directly to the right of (−2, −4). This right triangle has legs of 5 (the change from −2 to 3) and 12 (the change from −4 to 8). We can plug those values into the Pythagorean Theorem and solve for the hypotenuse:

$$A^2 + B^2 = C^2$$
$$5^2 + 12^2 = C^2$$
$$25 + 144 = C^2$$
$$C^2 = 169$$
$$C = \sqrt{169} = 13$$

Alternatively, we could recognize the common Pythagorean triplet 5, 12, 13.

Problem Set

1.   A line has the equation $y = 3x + 7$. At which point will this line intersect the y-axis?

2.   A line has the equation $x = \dfrac{y}{80} - 20$. At which point will this line intersect the x-axis?

3   A line has the equation $x = -2y + z$. If (3, 2) is a point on the line, what is z?

4.   A line is represented by the equation $y = zx + 18$. If this line intersects the x-axis at (−3, 0), what is z?

5.   A line has a slope of 1/6 and intersects the x-axis at (−24, 0). Where does this line intersect the y-axis?

6.   Which quadrants, if any, do not contain any points on the line represented by $x - y = 18$?

7.   Which quadrants, if any, do not contain any points on the line represented by $x = 10y$?

8.   Which quadrants, if any, contain points on the line $y = \dfrac{x}{1,000} + 1,000,000$?

9.   Which quadrants, if any, contain points on the line represented by $x + 18 = 2y$?

10.   What is the equation of the line shown to the right?

11.   What is the intersection point of the lines defined by the equations $2x + y = 7$ and $3x - 2y = 21$?

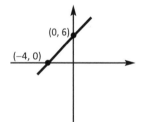

12.

Column A	Column B
The y-intercept of the line	The x-intercept of the line
$y = \dfrac{3}{2}x - 2$	$y = \dfrac{3}{2}x - 2$

13.

Column A	Column B
The slope of the line $2x + 5y = 10$	The slope of the line $5x + 2y = 10$

14.

Column A	Column B
The distance between points (0, −9) and (−2, 0)	The distance between points (3, 9) and (10, 3)

1. **(0, 7):** A line intersects the y-axis at the y-intercept. Since this equation is written in slope-intercept form, the y-intercept is easy to identify: 7. Thus, the line intersects the y-axis at the point (0, 7).

2. **(−20, 0) :** A line intersects the x-axis at the x-intercept, or when the y-coordinate is equal to zero. Substitute zero for y and solve for x:

$$x = 0 - 20$$
$$x = -20$$

3. **7:** Substitute the coordinates (3, 2) for x and y and solve for z.

$$3 = -2(2) + z$$
$$3 = -4 + z$$
$$z = 7$$

4. **6:** Substitute the coordinates (3, 2) for x and y and solve for z.

$$0 = z(-3) + 18$$
$$3z = 18$$
$$z = 6$$

5. **(0, 4):** Use the information given to find the equation of the line:

$$y = \frac{1}{6}x + b$$

$$0 = \frac{1}{6}(-24) + b$$

$$0 = -4 + b$$
$$b = 4$$

The variable b represents the y-intercept. Therefore, the line intersects the y-axis at (0, 4).

6. **II:** First, rewrite the line in slope-intercept form:

$$y = x - 18$$

Find the intercepts by setting x to zero and y to zero:

$$y = 0 - 18 \qquad\qquad 0 = x - 18$$
$$y = -18 \qquad\qquad x = 18$$

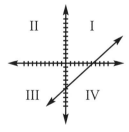

Plot the points: (0, −18), and (18, 0). From the sketch, we can see that the line does not pass through quadrant II.

7. **II and IV:** First, rewrite the line in slope-intercept form:

$$y = \frac{x}{10}$$

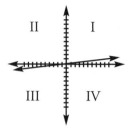

Notice from the equation that the *y*-intercept of the line is (0,0). This means that the line crosses the *y*-intercept at the origin, so the *x*- and *y*-intercepts are the same. To find another point on the line, substitute any convenient number for *x*; in this case, 10 would be a convenient, or "smart," number.

$$y = \frac{10}{10} = 1 \qquad \text{The point (10, 1) is on the line.}$$

Plot the points: (0, 0) and (10, 1). From the sketch, we can see that the line does not pass through quadrants II and IV.

8. **I, II, and III:** First, rewrite the line in slope-intercept form:

$$y = \frac{x}{1,000} + 1,000,000$$

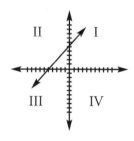

Find the intercepts by setting *x* to zero and *y* to zero:

$$0 = \frac{x}{1,000} + 1,000,000 \qquad y = \frac{0}{1,000} + 1,000,000$$

$$x = -1,000,000,000 \qquad y = 1,000,000$$

Plot the points: (−1,000,000,000, 0) and (0, 1,000,000). From the sketch, we can see that the line passes through quadrants I, II, and III.

9. **I, II, and III:** First, rewrite the line in slope-intercept form:

$$y = \frac{x}{2} + 9$$

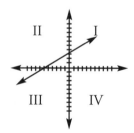

Find the intercepts by setting *x* to zero and *y* to zero:

$$0 = \frac{x}{2} + 9 \qquad y = \frac{0}{2} + 9$$

$$x = -18 \qquad y = 9$$

Plot the points: (−18, 0) and (0, 9). From the sketch, we can see that the line passes through quadrants I, II, and III.

10. $y = \dfrac{3}{2}x + 6$: First, calculate the slope of the line:

$$\text{slope} = \frac{\text{rise}}{\text{run}} = \frac{6-0}{0-(-4)} = \frac{6}{4} = \frac{3}{2}$$

We can see from the graph that the line crosses the *y*-axis at (0,6). The equation of the line is:

$$y = \frac{3}{2}x + 6$$

11. **(5, −3):** To find the coordinates of the point of intersection, solve the system of 2 linear equations. You could turn both equations into slope-intercept form and set them equal to each other, but it is easier is to multiply the first equation by 2 and then add the second equation:

$2x + y = 7$ (first equation) $7x = 35$ (sum of previous two equations)

$4x + 2y = 14$ (multiply by 2) $x = 5$

$3x − 2y = 21$ (second equation)

Now plug $x = 5$ into either equation:

$2x + y = 7$ (first equation) $10 + y = 7$

$2(5) + y = 7$ $y = −3$

Thus, the point (5, −3) is the point of intersection. There is no need to graph the two lines and find the point of intersection manually.

12. **B:**

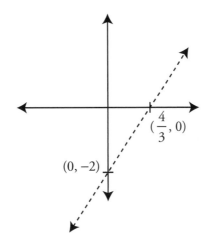

We've illustrated the line on the coordinate plane above. Because the equation is already in slope intercept form ($y = mx + b$), you can read the y-intercept directly from the b position, and use the slope to determine the x-intercept. A slope of 3/2 means that the line corresponding to this equation will rise 3 for every 2 that it runs. You don't need to determine the exact x-intercept to see that it is positive, and so greater than −2.

Alternatively, you could set each variable equal to 0, and determine the intercepts.

To determine the y-intercept, set x equal to 0, then solve for y:

$$y = \frac{3}{2}x − 2$$

$$y = \frac{3}{2}(0) − 2$$

$$y = 0 − 2 = −2$$

To determine the *x*-intercept, set *y* equal to 0, then solve for *x*:

$$y = \frac{3}{2}x - 2$$

$$(0) = \frac{3}{2}x - 2$$

$$2 = \frac{3}{2}x$$

$$\frac{4}{3} = x$$

Column A	**Column B**
The *y*-intercept of the line	The *x*-intercept of the line
$y = \frac{3}{2}x - 2 = \mathbf{-2}$	$y = \frac{3}{2}x - 2 = \mathbf{-\frac{4}{3}}$

13. **A:** The best method would be to put each equation into slope-intercept form ($y = mx + b$), and see which has the greater value for *m*, which represents the slope. Start with the equation **in Column A:**

$$2x + 5y = 10$$
$$5y = - +2x + 10$$
$$y = -\frac{2}{5}x + 2$$

Column A	**Column B**
The slope of the line	The slope of the line
$2x + 5y = 10 = \mathbf{-2/5}$	$5x + 2y = 10$

Now find the slope of the equation in **Column B:**

$$5x + 2y = 10$$
$$2y = -5x + 10$$
$$y = -\frac{5}{2}x + 5$$

Column A	**Column B**
$-2/5$	The slope of the line
	$5x + 2y = 10 = \mathbf{-5/2}$

Be careful. Remember that $-\frac{2}{5} > -\frac{5}{2}$.

*Manhattan*GRE®Prep
the new standard

14. **C:**

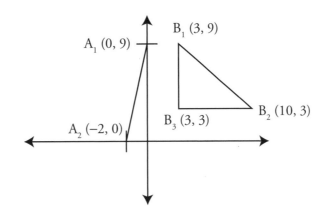

The illustration above shows the two points from **Column A,** here labeled A_1 and A_2, and the two points from **Column B,** here labeled B_1 and B_2. We have constructed a right triangle from the A values by finding a point $(0, 0)$ directly below A_1 and directly to the right of A_2. This right triangle has legs of 2 (the change from −2 to 0) and 9 (the change from 0 to 9). We can plug those values into the Pythagorean Theorem and solve for the hypotenuse:

$$A^2 + B^2 = C^2$$
$$(2)^2 + (9)^2 = C^2$$
$$4 + 81 = C^2$$
$$C^2 = 85$$
$$C = \sqrt{85}$$

Column A	**Column B**
The distance between points $(0, -9)$ and $(-2, 0) = \sqrt{\mathbf{85}}$	The distance between points $(3, 9)$ and $(10, 3)$

We have constructed a right triangle from the B values by finding a point $(3, 3)$ directly below B_1 and directly to the left of B_2. We have labeled this point B_3. This right triangle has legs of 7 (the change from 3 to 10) and 6 (the change from 3 to 9). We can plug those values into the Pythagorean Theorem and solve for the hypotenuse:

$$A^2 + B^2 = C^2$$
$$(7)^2 + (6)^2 = C^2$$
$$49 + 36 = C^2$$
$$C^2 = 85$$
$$C = \sqrt{85}$$

Column A	**Column B**
$\sqrt{85}$	The distance between points $(3, 9)$ and $(10, 3) = \sqrt{\mathbf{85}}$

g

Chapter 7
of
GEOMETRY

DRILL SETS

In This Chapter . . .

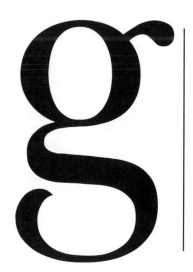

- Geometry Drill Sets

Geometry Drill Sets

DRILL SET 1:

Drill 1
1. The radius of a circle is 4. What is its area?
2. The diameter of a circle is 7. What is its circumference?
3. The radius of a circle is 3. What is its circumference?
4. The area of a circle is 36π. What is its radius?
5. The circumference of a circle is 18π. What is its area?

Drill 2
1. The area of a circle is 100π. What is its circumference?
2. The diameter of a circle is 16. Calculate its radius, circumference, and area.
3. Which circle has a larger area? Circle A has a circumference of 6π and Circle B has an area of 8π.
4. Which has a larger area? Circle C has a diameter of 10 and Circle D has a circumference of 12π.
5. A circle initially has an area of 4π. If the radius is doubled, the new area is how many times as large as the original area?

Drill 3
1. A sector has a central angle of 90°. If the sector has a radius of 8, what is the area of the sector?
2. A sector has a central angle of 30°. If the sector has a radius of 6, what is the arc length of the sector?
3. A sector has an arc length of 7π and a radius of 7. What is the central angle of the sector?
4. A sector has a central angle of 270°. If the sector has a radius of 4, what is the area of the sector?
5. A sector has an area of 24π and a radius of 12. What is the central angle of the sector?

Drill 4
1. The area of a sector is 1/10th the area of the full circle. What is the central angle of the sector?
2. What is the perimeter of a sector with a radius of 5 and a central angle of 72°?
3. A sector has a radius of 8 and an area of 8π. What is the arc length of the sector?
4. A sector has an arc length of $\pi/2$ and a central angle of 45°. What is the radius of the sector?
5. Which of the following two sectors has a larger area? Sector A has a radius of 4 and a central angle of 90°. Sector B has a radius of 6 and a central angle of 45°.

DRILL SET 2:

Drill 1
1. A triangle has two sides with lengths of 5 and 11, respectively. What is the range of values for the length of the third side?
2. In a right triangle, the length of one of the legs is 3 and the length of the hypotenuse is 5. What is the length of the other leg?

3. What is the area of Triangle *DEF*?

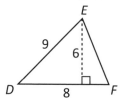

4. Which side of Triangle *GHI* has the longest length?

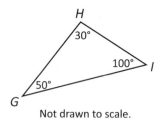

Not drawn to scale.

5. What is the value of *x*?

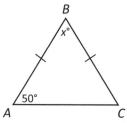

Not drawn to scale.

Drill 2

1. Two sides of a triangle have lengths 4 and 8. Which of the following are possible side lengths of the third side? (More than one may apply)

    a. 2   b. 4   c. 6   d. 8

2. *DFG* is a straight line. What is the value of *x*?

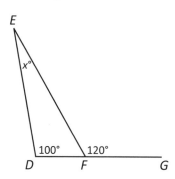

3. Isosceles triangle *ABC* has two sides with lengths 3 and 9. What is the length of the third side?

4. Which of the following could be the length of side *AB*, if $x < y < z$?

   a. 6   b. 10   c. 14

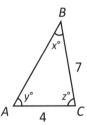

5. What is the area of right triangle *ABC*?

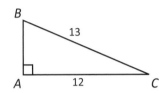

Drill 3

1. What is the perimeter of triangle *ABC*?

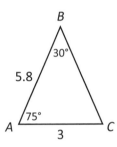

2. The area of right triangle *ABC* is 15. What is the length of hypotenuse *BC*?

3. What is the length of side *HI*?

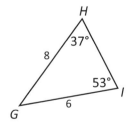

4. Which triangle has the greatest perimeter?

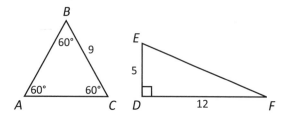

5. *WZ* has a length of 3 and *ZX* has a length of 6. What is the area of Triangle *XYZ*?

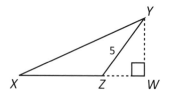

DRILL SET 3

Drill 1:

1. What is the perimeter of parallelogram *ABCD*?

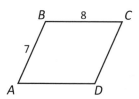

2. What is the area of parallelogram *EFGH*?

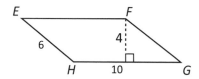

3. The two parallelograms pictured below have the same perimeter. What is the length of side *EH*?

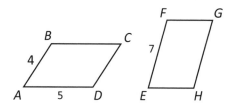

4. In Parallelogram *ABCD*, Triangle *ABC* has an area of 12. What is the area of Triangle *ACD*?

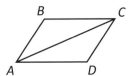

5. Rectangle *WXYZ* and Rectangle *OPQR* have equal areas. What is the length of side *PQ*?

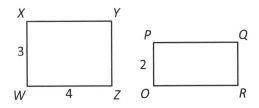

Drill 2

1. What is the area of Rectangle *ABCD*?

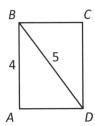

2. In Rectangle *ABCD*, the area of Triangle *ABC* is 30. What is the length of diagonal *AC*?

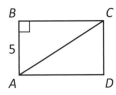

3. Rectangles *ABCD* and *EFGH* have equal areas. What is the length of side *FG*?

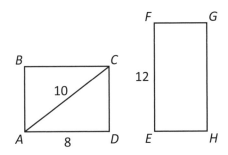

4. A rectangle has a perimeter of 10 and an area of 6. What are the length and width of the rectangle?

5. Triangle *XYZ* and Rectangle *JKLM* have equal areas. What is the perimeter of Rectangle *JKLM*?

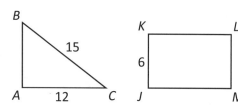

Drill 3

1. What is the perimeter of a square with an area of 25?

2. A rectangle and a square have the same area. The square has a perimeter of 32 and the rectangle has a length of 4. What is the width of the rectangle?

3. A circle is inscribed inside a square, so that the circle touches all four sides of the square. The length of one of the sides of the square is 9. What is the area of the circle?

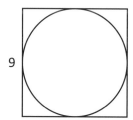

4. Square *ABCD* has an area of 49. What is the length of diagonal *AC*?

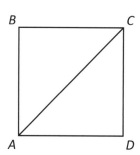

5. Right Triangle ABC and Rectangle *EFGH* have the same perimeter. What is the value of *x*?

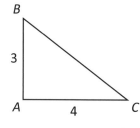
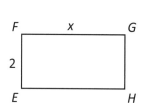

<u>DRILL SET 4:</u>

Drill 1

1. Draw a coordinate plane and plot the following points:

    1. (2, 3)   2. (−2, −1)   3. (−5, −6)   4. (4, −2.5)

2. What are the *x*- and *y*-coordinates of the following points?

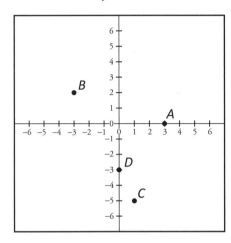

3. What is the *y*-coordinate of the point on the line that has an *x*-coordinate of 3?

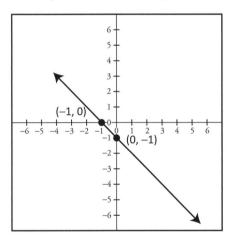

4. What is the *x*-coordinate of the point on the line that has a *y*-coordinate of −4?

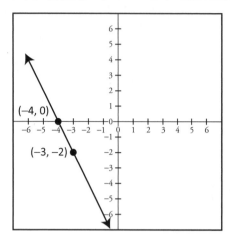

5. Does the point (3, −2) lie on the line $y = 2x - 8$?

Drill 2
1. Does the point (−3, 0) lie on the curve $y = x^2 - 3$?
2. For the line $y = 4x + 2$, what is the *y*-coordinate when $x = 3$?
3. What is the *y*-intercept of the line $y = -2x - 7$?
4. Graph the line $y = \dfrac{1}{3}x - 4$.

5. Graph the line $\dfrac{1}{2}y = -\dfrac{1}{2}x + 1$.

Drill Set Answers

DRILL SET 1:

Set 1, Drill 1

1. **16π:** The radius of a circle is 4. What is its area?

    Area of a circle is πr^2, so the area of the circle is $\pi(4)^2$, which equals 16π.

2. **7π:** The diameter of a circle is 7. What is its circumference?

    Circumference of a circle is $2\pi r$, or πd. We have the diameter, so the circumference equals $\pi(7)$, which equals 7π.

3. **6π:** The radius of a circle is 3. What is its circumference?

    Circumference of a circle is $2\pi r$, or πd. We have the radius, so circumference equals $2\pi(3)$, which equals 6π.

4. **6:** The area of a circle is 36π. What is its radius?

    Area of a circle is πr^2, so $36\pi = \pi r^2$. We need to solve for r. Divide both sides by π, so $36 = r^2$. Take the square root of both sides, and $6 = r$. We can ignore the negative solution because distances cannot be negative.

5. **81π:** The circumference of a circle is 18π. What is its area?

    The connection between circumference and area is radius. We can use the circumference to solve for the radius. $18\pi = 2\pi r$, which means that $9 = r$. That means that area $= \pi(9)^2$, which equals 81π.

Set 1, Drill 2

1. **20π:** The area of a circle is 100π. What is its circumference?

    The connection between circumference and area is radius. $100\pi = \pi r^2$, and solving for r gives us $r = 10$. That means that Circumference $= 2\pi(10)$, which equals 20π.

2. **64π:** The diameter of a circle is 16. Calculate its radius, circumference, and area.

    $d = 2r$, so $16 = 2r$. Radius $= 8$. Circumference $= 2\pi r$, so Circumference $= 2\pi(8) = 16\pi$. Area $= \pi r^2$, so Area $= \pi(8)^2 = 64\pi$.

3. **Circle A:** Which circle has a larger area? Circle A has a circumference of 6π and Circle B has an area of 8π.

    To figure out which circle has a larger area, we need to find the area of Circle A. If we know the circumference, then $6\pi = 2\pi r$, which means $r = 3$. If $r = 3$, then Area $= \pi(3)^2 = 9\pi$. $9\pi > 8\pi$, so Circle A has a larger area.

4. **Circle D:** Which has a larger area? Circle C has a diameter of 10 and Circle D has a circumference of 12π.

    We need to find the area of both circles. Let's start with Circle C. If the diameter of Circle C is 10, then the radius is 5. That means that Area $= \pi(5)^2 = 25\pi$.

If the circumference of Circle D is 12π, the $12\pi = 2\pi r$. $r = 6$. If $r = 6$, then Area $= \pi(6)^2 = 36\pi$. $36\pi > 25\pi$, so Circle D has the larger area.

5. **4 times:** A circle initially has an area of 4π. If the radius is doubled, the new area is how many times as large as the original area?

To begin, we need to find the original radius of the circle. $4\pi = \pi r^2$, so $r = 2$. If we double the radius, the new radius is 4. A circle with a radius of 4 has an area of 16π. 16π is 4 times 4π, so the new area is 4 times the original area.

Set 1, Drill 3

1. **16π:** A sector has a central angle of 90°. If the sector has a radius of 8, what is the area of the sector?

If the sector has a central angle of 90°, then the sector is 1/4 of the circle, because $\dfrac{90}{360} = \dfrac{1}{4}$. To find the area of the sector, we need to find the area of the whole circle first. The radius is 8, which means the area is $\pi(8)^2 = 64\pi$. $1/4 \times 64\pi = 16\pi$. The area of the sector is 16π.

2. **π:** A sector has a central angle of 30°. If the sector has a radius of 6, what is the arc length of the sector?

If the sector has a central angle of 30°, then it is 1/12th of the circle, because $\dfrac{30}{360} = \dfrac{1}{12}$. To find the arc length of the sector, we need to know the circumference of the entire circle. The radius of the circle is 6, so the circumference is $2\pi(6) = 12\pi$. That means that the arc length of the sector is $1/12 \times 12\pi = \pi$.

3. **180°:** A sector has an arc length of 7π and a radius of 7. What is the central angle of the sector?

To find the central angle of the sector, we first need to find what fraction of the full circle the sector is. We have the arc length, so if we can find the circumference of the circle, we can figure out what fraction of the circle the sector is. The radius is 7, so the circumference is $2\pi(7) = 14\pi$. $\dfrac{7\pi}{14\pi} = \dfrac{1}{2}$. So the sector is 1/2 the full circle. That means that the central angle of the sector is $1/2 \times 360° = 180°$. So the central angle is 180°.

4. **12π:** A sector has a central angle of 270°. If the sector has a radius of 4, what is the area of the sector?

The sector is 3/4 of the circle, because $\dfrac{270°}{360°} = \dfrac{3}{4}$. To find the area of the sector, we need the area of the whole circle. The radius of the circle is 4, so the area is $\pi(4)^2 = 16\pi$. That means the area of the circle is $3/4 \times 16\pi = 12\pi$.

5. **60°:** A sector has an area of 24π and a radius of 12. What is the central angle of the sector?

We first need to find the area of the whole circle. The radius is 12, which means the area is $\pi(12)^2 = 144\pi$. $\dfrac{24\pi}{144\pi} = \dfrac{1}{6}$, so the sector is 1/6th of the entire circle. That means that the central angle is 1/6th of 360. $1/6 \times 360 = 60$, so the central angle is 60°.

Set 1, Drill 4

1. **36°:** The area of a sector is 1/10th the area of the full circle. What is the central angle of the sector?

   If the area of the sector is 1/10th of the area of the full circle, then the central angle will be 1/10th of the degree measure of the full circle. $1/10 \times 360 = 36$, so the central angle of the sector is 36°.

2. **10 + 2π:** What is the perimeter of a sector with a radius of 5 and a central angle of 72°?

   To find the perimeter of a sector, we need to know the radius of the circle and the arc length of the sector.

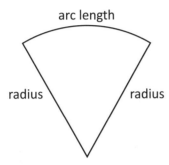

   We know the radius is 5, so now we need to find the arc length. Let's begin by determining what fraction of the circle the sector is. The central angle of the sector is 72°, so the sector is 1/5th of the circle, because $\dfrac{72}{360} = \dfrac{1}{5}$. Now we need to find the circumference. The radius is 5, so the circumference of the circle is $2\pi(5) = 10\pi$. The arc length of the sector is 1/5th the circumference. $1/5 \times 10\pi = 2\pi$. So now our sector looks like this. The perimeter of the sector is $10 + 2\pi$.

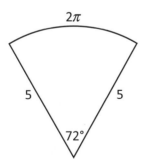

3. **2π:** A sector has a radius of 8 and an area of 8π. What is the arc length of the sector?

   We first need to find what fraction of the circle the sector is. We can do this by comparing areas. The radius of the circle is 8, so the area of the circle is $\pi(8)^2 = 64\pi$. That means the sector is 1/8th of the circle, because $\dfrac{8\pi}{64\pi} = \dfrac{1}{8}$. If we want to find the arc length of the sector, we need to know the circumference. The radius is 8, so the circumference is $2\pi(8) = 16\pi$. The sector is 1/8th of the circle, so the arc length will be 1/8th of the circumference. $1/8 \times 16\pi = 2\pi$. The arc length of the sector is 2π.

4. 2: A sector has an arc length of $\pi/2$ and a central angle of 45°. What is the radius of the sector?

If the sector has a central angle of 45°, then the sector is 1/8th of the circle, because $\dfrac{45}{360} = \dfrac{1}{8}$. If the sector is 1/8th of the circle, then that means the arc length of the sector is 1/8th of the circumference of the circle. That means that $\pi/2$ is 1/8th of the circumference. If we designate x as the circumference of the circle, then we can say that $\dfrac{\pi}{2} = \dfrac{1}{8}x$. Multiply both sides by 8, and we get $4\pi = x$. That means the circumference is 4π. We know the formula for circumference, so we know that $4\pi = 2\pi r$. Divide both sides by 2π and we get $r = 2$. The radius of the sector is 2.

5. Sector B: Which of the following two sectors has a larger area? Sector A has a radius of 4 and a central angle of 90°. Sector B has a radius of 6 and a central angle of 45°.

We need to find the area of each circle. Sector A is 1/4th of the circle, because $\dfrac{90}{360} = \dfrac{1}{4}$. The radius is 4, so the area of the circle is $\pi(4)^2 = 16\pi$. That means the area of Sector A is 1/4th of 16π. $1/4 \times 16\pi = 4\pi$, so the area of Sector A is 4π.

Sector B is 1/8th of the circle, because $\dfrac{45}{360} = \dfrac{1}{8}$. The radius of Sector B is 8, so the area of the full circle is $\pi(6)^2 = 36\pi$. Sector B is 1/8th of the circle, so the area of Sector B is $1/8 \times 36\pi = 4.5\pi$. The area of Sector B is 4.5π.

$4.5\pi > 4\pi$, so the area of Sector B is greater than the area of Sector A.

DRILL SET 2:

Set 2, Drill 1

1. 6 < third side < 16.: A triangle has two sides with lengths of 5 and 11, respectively. What is the range of values for the length of the third side?

The lengths of any two sides of a triangle must add up to more than the length of the third side. The third side must be less than $5 + 11 = 16$. It must also be greater than $11 - 5 = 6$. Therefore, 6 < third side < 16.

2. 4: In a right triangle, the length of one of the legs is 3 and the length of the hypotenuse is 5. What is the length of the other leg?

If you know the lengths of two sides of a right triangle, you can use the Pythagorean Theorem to solve for the length of the third side. Remember that the hypotenuse must be the side labeled c in the equation $a^2 + b^2 = c^2$. That means that $(3)^2 + (b)^2 = (5)^2$. $9 + b^2 = 25$. $b^2 = 16$, so $b = 4$.

Alternatively, you can recognize the Pythagorean triplet. This is a 3–4–5 triangle.

3. **24:** What is the area of Triangle *DEF*?

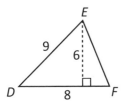

The area of a triangle is ¹/₂ base × height. Remember that the base and the height must be perpendicular to each other. That means that in Triangle *DEF*, side *DF* can act as the base, and the line dropping straight down from point *E* to touch side *DF* at a right angle can act as the base. Therefore Area = ¹/₂ (8) × (6) = 24.

4. **Side *GH*:** Which side of Triangle *GHI* has the longest length?

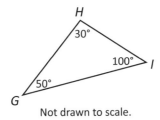

Not drawn to scale.

Although *GI* looks like the longest side, remember that you can't trust what the picture looks like when the question states the picture is not drawn to scale. In any triangle, the longest side will be opposite the largest angle. Angle *GIH* is the largest angle in the triangle, and side *GH* is thus the longest side.

5. **80:** What is the value of *x*?

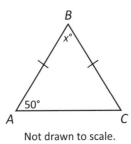

Not drawn to scale.

If you know the other 2 angles in a triangle, then you can find the third, because all 3 angles must add up to 180. In Triangle *ABC*, sides *AB* and *BC* are equal. That means their opposite angles are also equal. That means that angle *ACB* is also 50°.

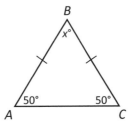

Now that we know the other 2 angles, we can find angle *x*. We know that 50 + 50 + *x* = 180, so *x* = 80.

Set 2, Drill 2

1. **c & d:** Two sides of a triangle have lengths 4 and 8. Which of the following are possible side lengths of the third side? (More than one may apply)

   a. 2   b. 4   c. 6   d. 8

   The lengths of any two sides of a triangle must add up to more than the length of the third side. The third side must be less than $4 + 8 = 12$ and greater than $8 - 4 = 4$. So $4 <$ third side < 12. Only choices c. and d. are in that range.

2. **20:** *DFG* is a straight line. What is the value of x?

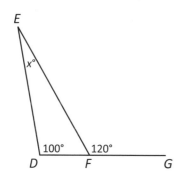

   To find the value of x, we need to find the degree measures of the other two angles in Triangle *DEF*. We can make use of the fact that *DFG* is a straight line. Straight lines have a degree measure of 180, so angle *DFE* $+ 120 = 180$, which means angle *DFE* $= 60$.

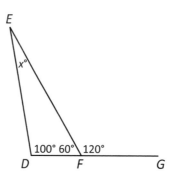

   Now we can solve for x, because $100 + 60 + x = 180$. Solving for x, we get $x = 20$.

3. **9:** Isosceles triangle *ABC* has two sides with lengths 3 and 9. What is the length of the third side?

   It may at first appear like we don't have enough information to answer this question. If all we know is that the triangle is isosceles, then all we know is that two sides have equal length, which means the third side has a length of either 3 or 9. But if the third side were 3, then the lengths of two of the sides would not add up to greater than the length of the third side, because $3 + 3$ is not greater than 9.

   That means that the length of the third side must be 9.

4. **b:** Which of the following could be the length of side *AB*, if $x < y < z$?

   a. 6   b. 10   c. 14

Manhattan **GRE**®**Prep**
the new standard

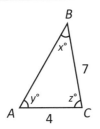

There are two properties of a triangle at play here. The lengths of any two sides of a triangle must add up to greater than the length of the third side. Also, longer sides must be opposite larger angles. Answer choice a. is out because side *AB* is opposite the largest angle, so side *AB* must have a length greater than 7. Answer choice c. is out, because $4 + 7 = 11$, so the third side has to be less than 11. The only remaining possibility is b. 10.

5. **30:** What is the area of right triangle *ABC*?

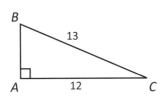

To find the area, we need a base and a height. If we can find the length of side *AB*, then *AB* can be the height and *AC* can be the base, because the two sides are perpendicular to each other.

We can use the Pythagorean Theorem to find the length of side *AB*. $(a)^2 + (12)^2 = (13)^2$. $a^2 + 144 = 169$. $a^2 = 25$. $a = 5$. Alternatively, we could recognize that the triangle is a Pythagorean triplet 5–12–13.

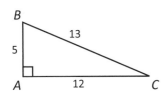

Now that we know the length of side *AB* we can find the area. Area $= \frac{1}{2}(12) \times (5) = 30$.

Set 2, Drill 3

1. **14.6:** What is the perimeter of triangle *ABC*?

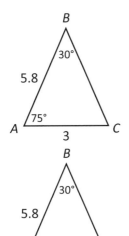

To find the perimeter of Triangle *ABC*, we need the lengths of all 3 sides. There is no immediately obvious way to find the length of side *BC*, so let's see what inferences we can make from the information the question gave us.

We know the degree measures of two of the angles in Triangle *ABC*, so we can find the degree measure of the third. We'll label the third angle *x*. We know that $30 + 75 + x = 180$. Solving for *x* we find that $x = 75$.

Angle *BAC* and angle *BCA* are both 75, which means Triangle *ABC* is an isosceles triangle. If those two angles are equal, we know that their opposite sides are also equal. Side *AB* has a length of 5.8, so we know that *BC* also has a length of 5.8.

To find the perimeter, we add up the lengths of the three sides. $4 + 4 + 3 = 11$.

2. $\sqrt{61}$: The area of right triangle ABC is 15. What is the length of hypotenuse BC?

To find the length of the hypotenuse, we need the lengths of the other two sides. Then we can use the Pythagorean Theorem to find the length of the hypotenuse. We can use the area formula to find the length of AC. Area = $\frac{1}{2}$ base × height, and we know the area and the height. So $15 = \frac{1}{2}$ (base) × (5). When we solve this equation, we find that the base = 6.

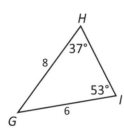

Now we can use the Pythagorean Theorem. $(5)^2 + (6)^2 = c^2$. $25 + 36 = c^2$. $61 = c^2$. $\sqrt{61} = c$. Since 61 is not a perfect square, we know that c will be a decimal. 61 is also prime, so we cannot simplify $\sqrt{61}$ any further. (It will be a little less than $\sqrt{64} = 8$.)

3. **10:** What is the length of side HI?

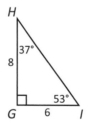

There is no immediately obvious way to find the length of side HI, so let's see what we can infer from the picture. We know two of the angles of Triangle GHI, so we can find the third. We'll label the third angle x. $40 + 50 + x = 180$. That means $x = 90$. So really our triangle looks like this:

You should definitely redraw once you discover the triangle is a right triangle!

Now that we know Triangle GHI is a right triangle, we can use the Pythagorean Theorem to find the length of HI. HI is the hypotenuse, so $(6)^2 + (8)^2 = c^2$. $36 + 64 = c^2$. $100 = c^2$. $10 = c$. The length of HI is 10.

Alternatively, we could have recognized the Pythagorean triplet. Triangle GHI is a 6–8–10 triangle.

4. **Triangle *DEF*:** Which triangle has the greater perimeter?

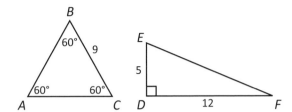

To determine which triangle has the greater perimeter, we need to know the side lengths of all three sides of both triangles. Let's begin with Triangle *ABC*.

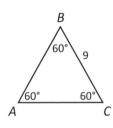

All three angles in Triangle *ABC* are 60°. If all three angles are equal, that means all three sides are equal in this equilateral triangle. So every side of Triangle *ABC* has a length of 9. That means the perimeter = 9 + 9 + 9 = 27.

Now let's look at Triangle *DEF*. Triangle *DEF* is a right triangle, so we can use the Pythagorean Theorem to find the length of side *EF*. *EF* is the hypotenuse, so $(5)^2 + (12)^2 = c^2$. $25 + 144 = c^2$. $169 = c^2$. $13 = c$. That means the perimeter is 5 + 12 + 13 = 30. Alternatively, 5–12–13 is a Pythagorean triplet.

30 > 27, so Triangle *DEF* has a greater perimeter than Triangle *ABC*.

5. **12:** *WZ* has a length of 3 and *ZX* has a length of 6. What is the area of Triangle *XYZ*?

Let's start by filling in everything we know about Triangle *XYZ*.

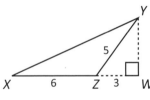

To find the area of Triangle *XYZ*, we need a base and a height. If Side *XZ* is a base, then *YW* can act as a height. We can find the length of *YW* because Triangle *ZYW* is a right triangle, and we know the lengths of two of the sides. *YZ* is the hypotenuse, so $(a)^2 + (3)^2 = (5)^2$. $a^2 + 9 = 25$. $a^2 = 16$. $a = 4$.

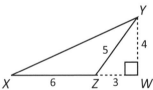

Alternatively, we could recognize the Pythagorean triplet: *ZYW* is a 3–4–5 triangle.

Now we know that the area of Triangle *XYZ* is $\frac{1}{2}b \times h = \frac{1}{2}(6) \times (4) = 12$.

DRILL SET 3:

Set 3, Drill 1

1. **30:** What is the perimeter of parallelogram *ABCD*?

Opposite sides of a parallelogram are equal, so we know that side *CD* has a length of 7 and side *AD* has a length of 8. So the perimeter is 7 + 8 + 7 + 8 = 30.

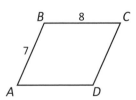

Alternatively, the perimeter is $2 \times (7 + 8) = 30$. We can say this because we know that 2 sides have a length of 7 and 2 sides have a length of 8.

2. **40:** What is the area of parallelogram *EFGH*?

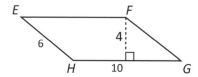

The area of a parallelogram is base × height. In this parallelogram, the base is 10 and the height is 4 (remember, base and height need to be perpendicular). So the area is $10 \times 4 = 40$.

3. **2:** The two parallelograms pictured below have the same perimeter. What is the length of side *EH*?

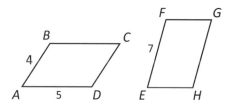

First we can find the perimeter of Parallelogram *ABCD*. We know that 2 sides have a length of 4, and 2 sides have a length of 5. The perimeter is $2 \times (4 + 5) = 18$. That means Parallelogram *EFGH* also has a perimeter of 18. We know side *GH* also has a length of 7. We don't know the lengths of the other 2 sides, but we know they have the same length, so for now let's say the length of each side is *x*. Our parallelogram now looks like this:

So we know that $7 + x + 7 + x = 18$ ➔ $2x + 14 = 18$ ➔ $2x = 4$ ➔ $x = 2$

The length of side *EH* is 2.

4. **12:** In Parallelogram *ABCD*, Triangle *ABC* has an area of 12. What is the area of Triangle *ACD*?

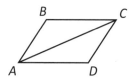

One property that is true of any parallelogram is that the diagonal will split the parallelogram into two equal triangles. If Triangle *ABC* has an area of 12, then Triangle *ACD* must also have an area of 12.

5. **6:** Rectangle *WXYZ* and Rectangle *OPQR* have equal areas. What is the length of side *PQ*?

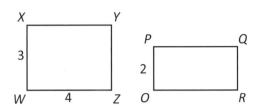

We can start by finding the area of Rectangle *WXYZ*. Area of a rectangle is length × width, so the area of Rectangle *WXYZ* is 3 × 4 = 12. So Rectangle *OPQR* also has an area of 12. We know the length of side *OP*, so that is the width of Rectangle *OPQR*. So now we know the area, and we know the width, so we can solve for the length. $l \times 2 = 12 \rightarrow l = 6$. The length of side *PQ* is 6.

Set 3, Drill 2

1. **12:** What is the area of Rectangle *ABCD*?

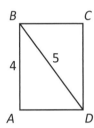

To find the area of Rectangle *ABCD*, we need to know the length of *AD* or *BC*. In a rectangle, every internal angle is 90 degrees, so Triangle *ABD* is actually a right triangle. That means we can use the Pythagorean Theorem to find the length of side *AD*. Actually, this right triangle is one of the Pythagorean Triplets—a 3–4–5 triangle. The length of side *AD* is 3. That means the area of Rectangle *ABCD* is 3 × 4 = 12.

2. **13:** In Rectangle *ABCD*, the area of Triangle *ABC* is 30. What is the length of diagonal *AC*?

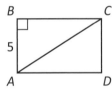

We know the area of Triangle *ABC* and the length of side *AB*. Because side *BC* is perpendicular to side *AB*, we can use those as the base and height of Triangle *ABC*. So we know that $^1/_2(5) \times (BC) = 30$. That means the length of side *BC* is 12.

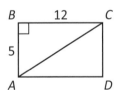

Now we can use the Pythagorean Theorem to find the length of diagonal *AC*, which is the hypotenuse of right triangle *ABC*. We can also recognize that this is a Pythagorean Triplet —a 5–12–13 triangle. The length of diagonal *AC* is 13.

3. **4:** Rectangles *ABCD* and *EFGH* have equal areas. What is the length of side *FG*?

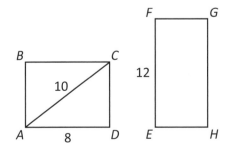

The first thing to notice in this problem is that we can find the length of side *CD*. Triangle *ACD* is a right triangle, and we know the lengths of two of the sides. We can either use the Pythagorean Theorem or recognize that this is one of our Pythagorean Triplets—a 6–8–10 triangle. The length of side *CD* is 6. Now we can find the area of Rectangle *ABCD*. Side *AD* is the length and side *CD* is the width. 8 × 6 = 48.

That means that the area of Rectangle *EFGH* is also 48. We can use the area and the length of side *EF* to solve for the length of side *FG*. $12 \times (FG) = 48$. The length of side *FG* is 4.

4. **length and width are 2 and 3:** A rectangle has a perimeter of 10 and an area of 6. What are the length and width of the rectangle?

In order to answer this question, let's begin by drawing a rectangle. In this rectangle, we'll make one pair of equal sides have a length of *x*, and the other pair of equal sides has a length of *y*.

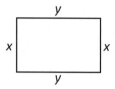

Using the lengths *x* and *y*, we know the perimeter of the rectangle is $2x + 2y$. So we know that:

$2x + 2y = 10$ This can be simplified to $\boldsymbol{x + y = 5}$.

We also know the area of the rectangle is $xy = 6$.

$\boldsymbol{xy = 6}$ Area of the rectangle $= l \times w = 6$

Now we can use substitution to solve for the values of our variables. In the first equation, we can isolate *x*.

$x = 5 - y$

Substitute $(5 - y)$ for *x* in the second equation.

$(5 - y)y = 6$
$5y - y^2 = 6$ This is a quadratic, so we need to get everything on one side.
$y^2 - 5y + 6 = 0$ Now we can factor the equation.
$(y - 3)(y - 2) = 0$

So $y = 2$ or 3.

When we plug in these values to solve for *x*, we find something a little unusual. When $y = 2$, $x = 3$. When $y = 3$, $x = 2$. What that means is that either the length is 2 and the width is 3, or the length is 3 and the width is 2. Both of these rectangles are identical, so we have our answer.

5. **30:** Triangle *XYZ* and Rectangle *JKLM* have equal areas. What is the perimeter of Rectangle *JKLM*?

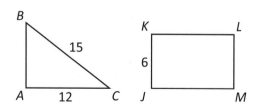

If we can find the length of side *AB*, then we can find the area of Triangle *ABC*. We can use the Pythagorean Theorem to find the length of side *AB*. $(12)^2 + (AB)^2 = (15)^2 \rightarrow 144 + AB^2 = 225 \rightarrow AB^2 = 81 \rightarrow AB = 9$. (A 9–12–15 triangle is a 3–4–5 triangle, with all the measurements tripled.)

*Manhattan*GRE* Prep
the new standard

Now that we know *AB*, we can find the area of Triangle *ABC*. It's $\frac{1}{2}(12) \times 9 = 54$.

That means that Rectangle *JKLM* also has an area of 54. We have one side of the rectangle, so we can solve for the other. $6 \times (JM) = 54$. So the length of side *JM* is 9. That means that the perimeter is $2 \times (6 + 9) = 30$.

Set 3, Drill 3

1. **20:** What is the perimeter of a square with an area of 25?

    A square has four equal sides, so the area of a square is the length of one side squared. That means the lengths of the sides of the square are 5. If each of the four sides has a length of 5, then the perimeter is $4 \times (5) = 20$.

2. **16:** A rectangle and a square have the same area. The square has a perimeter of 32 and the rectangle has a length of 4. What is the width of the rectangle?

    We should start by drawing the shapes that they describe.

    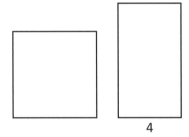

    The square has four equal sides, so that means that the perimeter is 4 times the length of one side. If we designate the length of the sides of the square *s*, then the perimeter is $4s = 32$. That means that *s* is 8. Now that we know the length of the sides, we can figure out the area of the square. Area $= 8^2$. So the area of the square is 64.

    That means that the area of the rectangle is also 64. We know the length of the rectangle is 4, so we can solve for the width. $4 \times (\text{width}) = 64$. The width is 16.

3. **20.25π:** A circle is inscribed inside a square, so that the circle touches all four sides of the square. The length of one of the sides of the square is 9. What is the area of the circle?

    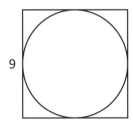

    We need to find a common link between the square and the circle, so that we can find the area of the circle. We know that the length of the sides of the square is 9. We can draw a new line in our figure that has the same length as the sides AND is the diameter of the circle.

    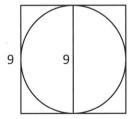

    That means that the diameter of the circle is 9. If the diameter is 9, then the radius is 4.5. That means the area of the circle is $\pi(4.5)^2$, which equals 20.25π.

4. $7\sqrt{2}$:   Square *ABCD* has an area of 49. What is the length of diagonal *AC*?

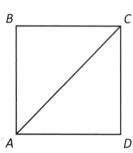

If the square has an area of 49, then (side)^2 = 49. That means that the length of the sides of the square is 7. So our square looks like this:

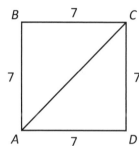

Now we can use the Pythagorean Theorem to find the length of diagonal *AC*, which is also the hypotenuse of Triangle *ACD*. $7^2 + 7^2 = (AC)^2$ → $98 = (AC)^2$ → $\sqrt{98} = AC$. But this can be simplified. $AC = \sqrt{2 \times 49} = \sqrt{2 \times 7 \times 7} = 7\sqrt{2}$.

5. **4:**   Right Triangle *ABC* and Rectangle *EFGH* have the same perimeter. What is the value of *x*?

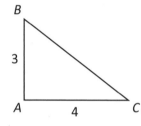 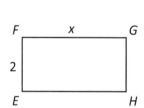

Triangle *ABC* is a right triangle, so we can find the length of hypotenuse *BC*. This is a 3–4–5 triangle, so the length of side *BC* is 5. That means the perimeter of Triangle *ABC* is 3 + 4 + 5 = 12.

That means the perimeter of Rectangle *EFGH* is also 12. That means that $2 \times (2 + x) = 12$. So 4 + $2x = 12$ → $2x = 8$ → $x = 4$.

DRILL SET 4:

Set 4, Drill 1

1.   Draw a coordinate plane and plot the following points:
      1. (2, 3)   2. (−2, −1)   3. (−5, −6)   4. (4, −2.5)

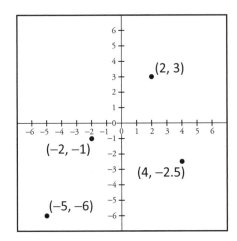

2.   *A*: (3, 0)   *B*: (−3, 2)   *C*: (1, −5)   *D*: (0, −3)

3.   The *y*-coordinate of the point on the line that has an *x*-coordinate of 3 is −4. The point is (3, −4).
      If you want, you can determine that the line has a slope of −1 from the two labeled points that the
      line intercepts, (−1, 0) and (0, −1).

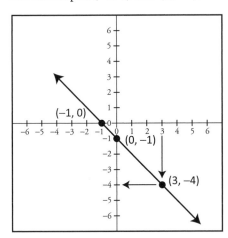

4. The *x*-coordinate of the point on the line that has a *y*-coordinate of −4 is −2. The point is (−2, −4). If you want, you can determine that the line has a slope of −2 from the two labeled points that the line intercepts, (−4, 0) and (−3, −2).

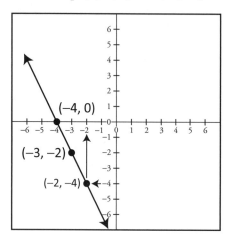

5. For the point (3, −2) to lie on the line $y = 2x − 8$, y needs to equal −2 when we plug in 3 for x.

$y = 2(3) − 8$
$y = 6 − 8 = −2$
y does equal −2 when x equals 3, so the point does lie on the line.

Set 4, Drill 2

1. For the point (−3, 0) to lie on the curve $y = x^2 − 3$, y needs to equal 0 when we plug in −3 for x.

$y = (−3)^2 − 3$
$y = 9 − 3 = 6$
y does not equal 0 when x equals −3, so the point does not lie on the curve.

2. To find the *y*-coordinate, we need to plug in 3 for x and solve for y.

$y = 4(3) + 2$
$y = 12 + 2 = 14$
The *y*-coordinate is 14. The point is (3, 14).

3. The equation of the line is already in $y = mx + b$ form, and b stands for the *y*-intercept, so we just need to look at the equation to find the *y*-intercept. The equation is $y = −2x − 7$. That means the *y*-intercept is −7. The point is (0, −7).

4.   Graph the line $y = \dfrac{1}{3}x - 4$

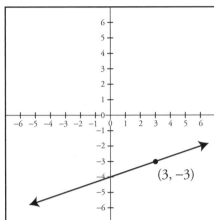

The slope (m) is 1/3, so the line slopes gently up to the right, rising only 1 unit for every 3 units of run.

The y-intercept (b) is −4, so the line crosses the y-axis at (0, −4).

5.   Graph the line $\dfrac{1}{2}y = -\dfrac{1}{2}x + 1$.

Before we can graph the line, we need to put the equation into $y = mx + b$ form. Multiply both sides by 2.

$y = -x + 2$

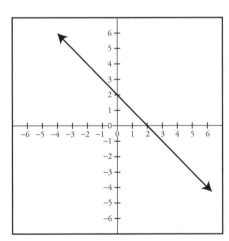

The slope (m) is −1, so the line drops to the right, falling 1 unit for every unit of run.

The y-intercept is 2, so the line crosses the y-axis at (0, 2).

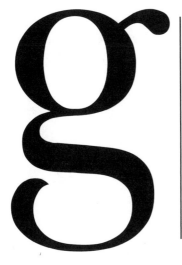

Appendix
of
GEOMETRY

2011 CHANGES TO THE GRE QUANT

In This Chapter . . .

- 2011 Changes to the GRE Quant
- Multiple Choice: Select One or More Answer Choices
- Numeric Entry
- Using the Calculator
- 2011 Format Math Questions

2011 Changes to the GRE Quant

In mid-2011, the Quantitative section of the GRE will undergo a number of changes. Have no fear, however—the actual body of mathematical knowledge being tested won't change, and everything in your Manhattan GRE book(s) will still be relevant and necessary to beat the test. This supplement details everything you need to know to be ready for 2011.

Currently, the GRE contains a single 45-minute quantitative section composed of multiple choice problems, Quantitative Comparisons, and Data Interpretation questions (which are really a subset of multiple choice problems).

After the 2011 changes, test takers will complete two separate 35-minute quantitative sections containing two new problem formats in addition to the current problem formats.

Additionally, a small four-function calculator with a square root will appear on-screen. Truly, many test takers will rejoice at the advent of this calculator! It is true that the GRE calculator will reduce emphasis on computation—but look out for problems in which the order of operations, or tricky wording on percents, is likely to foil those who rely on it too much.

New Problem Formats in Brief:

Multiple Choice: Select One or More Answer Choices – Questions may have from three to seven answer choices, and the test taker is asked to select a certain number of answers ("Which two of the following…") or to select all answers that meet a certain criterion ("Select all that apply").

Numeric Entry – Instead of selecting a multiple-choice answer, test takers type an answer into an entry box, or two entry boxes above and below a fraction bar.

Data Interpretation questions will also occur more often, and the above new problem types will also be used on Data Interpretation; that is, you will be presented with charts or graphs and asked a mix of Multiple Choice: Select One, Multiple Choice: Select One or More, and Numeric Entry questions.

We're about to discuss strategies for each new problem type. But overall, don't worry! The same core mathematical skills are being tested, and any time you've put into studying for the pre-2011 GRE will still be useful for the 2011 GRE. Also, as you're about to see, many of these problem types aren't as different as they might seem.

Finally, don't worry about whether these new problem types are "harder" or "easier." You're being judged against other students, all of whom are in the same boat. So if the new formats are harder, they're harder for other test takers as well. The upcoming strategies and problem sets will put you ahead of the game!

Multiple Choice: Select One or More Answer Choices

The official directions for "Select One or More Answer Choices" read as follows:

> Directions: Select one or more answer choices according to the specific question directions.
>
> If the question does not specify how many answer choices to select, select all that apply.
>
> The correct answer may be just one of the choices or as many as all of the choices, depending on the question.
>
> No credit is given unless you select all of the correct choices and no others.
>
> If the question specifies how many answer choices to select, select exactly that number of choices.

Note that there is no "partial credit." If three of six choices are correct and you select two of the three, no credit is given. It will also be important to read the directions carefully.

That said, many of these questions look *very* similar to those you've studied for the "old" GRE. For instance, here is a question that could have appeared on the GRE at any time:

If $ab = |a| \times |b|$, which of the following *must* be true?

    I. $a = b$
    II. $a > 0$ and $b > 0$
    III. $ab > 0$

    A.   II only
    B.   III only
    C.   I and III only
    D.   II and III only
    E.   I, II, and III

Solution: If $ab = |a| \times |b|$, then we know ab is positive, since the right side of the equation must be positive. If ab is positive, however, that doesn't necessarily mean that a and b are each positive; it simply means that they have the same sign.

    I.   It is not true that a must equal b. For instance, a could be 2 and b could be 3.
    II.   It is not true that a and b must each be positive. For instance, a could be −3 and b could be −4.
    III.   True. Since $|a| \times |b|$ must be positive, ab must be positive as well.

The answer is B (III only).

Note that, if you determined that statement I was false, you could eliminate choices C and E before considering the remaining statements. Then, if you were confident that II was also false, you could safely pick answer choice B, III only, without even trying statement III, since "None of the above" isn't an option.

That is, because of the multiple choice answers, it is sometimes not necessary to consider each statement individually. This is the aspect of such problems that will change on the 2011 exam.

Here is the same problem, in 2011 format.

> If $ab = |a| \times |b|$, which of the following *must* be true?
>
> Indicate <u>all</u> such statements.
>
> A. $a = b$
> B. $a > 0$ and $b > 0$
> C. $ab > 0$

Strategy Tip: Make sure to fully "process" the statement in the question (simplify it or list the possible scenarios) before considering the answer choices. This will save you time in the long run!

Here, we would simply select choice C. The only thing that has changed is that we can't do process of elimination; we must always consider each statement individually. On the upside, the problem has become much more straightforward and compact (not every real-life problem has exactly five possible solutions; why should those on the GRE?)

Numeric Entry

The official directions for "Numeric Entry" read as follows:

> Directions: Enter your answer in the answer box(es) below the question.
>
> Equivalent forms of the correct answer, such as 2.5 and 2.50, are all correct. Fractions do not need to be reduced to lowest terms.
>
> Enter the exact answer unless the question asks you to round your answer.

Strategy Tip: Note that you are not required to reduce fractions. It may feel strange to type 9/27 instead of 1/3, but if you're not required to reduce, why take an extra step that has the possibility of introducing a mistake?

In this problem type, you are not able to "work backwards" from answer choices, and in many cases it will be difficult to make a guess. However, the principles being tested are just the same as on the old GRE.

Here is a sample question:

> If $x*y = 2xy - (x - y)$, what is the value of $3*4$?

Solution:

We are given a function involving two variables, x and y, and asked to substitute 3 for x and 4 for y:

$x*y = 2xy - (x - y)$

$3*4 = 2(3)(4) - (3 - 4)$

$3*4 = 24 - (-1)$

$3*4 = 25$

The answer is 25.

Thus, you would type 25 into the box.

Using the Calculator

The addition of a small, four-function calculator with a square root means that those taking the 2011 test can forget re-memorizing their times tables or square roots. However, the calculator is not a cure-all; in many problems, the difficulty is in figuring out what numbers to put into the calculator in the first place. In some cases, using a calculator will actually be less helpful than doing the problem some other way.

On the new 2011 GRE, you will be provided with a simple on-screen calculator. For this practice set, you may use any calculator, but don't use any functions other than $+$, $-$, $\times$, $\div$, and $\sqrt{}$.

> If x is the remainder when (11)(7) is divided by 4 and y is the remainder when (14)(6) is divided by 13, what is the value of $x + y$?

Solution: This problem is designed so that the calculator won't tell the whole story. Certainly the calculator will tell us that $11 \times 7 = 77$. When you divide 77 by 4, however, the calculator yields an answer of 19.25. The remainder is *not* 0.25 (a remainder is always a whole number).

You might just go back to your pencil and paper, and find the largest multiple of 4 that is less than 77. Since 4 DOES go into 76, we can conclude that 4 would leave a remainder of 1 when dividing into 77. (Notice that we don't even need to know how many times 4 goes into 76, just that it goes in. One way to mentally "jump" to 76 is to say, *4 goes into 40, so it goes into 80... that's a bit too big, so take away 4 to get 76*).

However, it is also possible to use the calculator to find a remainder. Divide 77 by 4 to get 19.25. Thus, 4 goes into 77 nineteen times, with a remainder left over. Now use your calculator to multiply 19 (JUST 19, not 19.25) by 4. You will get 76. The remainder is $77 - 76 = 1$. Therefore, $x = 1$.

Use the same technique to find y. Multiply 14×6 to get 84. Divide 84 by 13 to get 6.46... Ignore everything after the decimal, and just multiply 6 by 13 to get 78. The remainder is therefore $84 - 78 = 6$. Therefore, $y = 6$.

Since we are looking for $x + y$ and $1 + 6 = 7$, the answer is 7.

2011 Format Geometry Questions

On the new 2011 GRE, you will be provided with a simple on-screen calculator. For this practice set, you may use any calculator, but don't use any functions other than +, −, ×, ÷, and $\sqrt{\ }$.

1.   If a circle's diameter is between 2 and 10, which of the following could be its area?

Indicate <u>all</u> such statements.

A. 3
B. 10π
C. 60

2.   If a square's length is increased by 20% and its width is increased by 50%, what is the ratio of its new area to its old area?

3.   On a number line, A is to the left of 0, B is to the right of 0, $\overline{AB} > 4$, and C is the midpoint of AB. Which THREE of the following MUST be true?

A. $\overline{AB} > 2$
B. $C = 0$
C. $\overline{AB} > 2\overline{AC}$
D. $\overline{AC} = 2$
E. A is at least 2 units to the left of 0
F. $\overline{AB} > \overline{AC}$
G. A is less than 2 units to the left of 0

4. A right triangle's sides have consecutive integer lengths. If the triangle's perimeter is less than 15, what is its area?

2011 GRE Quant Solutions:

1. **B & C:** If a circle's diameter is between 2 and 10, its RADIUS must be between 1 and 5. Thus, since $A = \pi r^2$, its area must be between 1π and 25π.

Note that some of the answer choices have π and some don't. Also note that there are no integer constraints in this problem—the radius could be something strange, like $\sqrt{5}$ or $12/\pi$, as long as the value is between 1 and 5 (which both of those examples are).

So the final step is simply to put 1π and 25π in the calculator to find that the area must be between about 3.14 and about 78.5. Thus, A is too small, but the others are valid.

The answer is B and C.

2. **9/5:** An easy way to do this problem is to make a 10 by 10 square. That's the "old" image. Its area is 100.

Now, the length is increased by 20% and the width is increased by 50%. Draw a rectangle with sides 12 and 15 (the benefit of starting with a 10 by 10 square is that it is very easy to increase 10 by a percent). Multiply 12 × 15 (use the calculator if you like) to get the new area, 180.

The question asks for the ratio of the new area to the old area. Put 180 over 100 and reduce.

The answer is 9/5.

3. **A, C, & E:** This is one shifty number line—we know A and B are more than 4 apart and that A is to the left of zero and B is to the right of zero—but we DON'T know that A and B are evenly spaced from zero. For instance, A could be −2 and B could be 98, which would put their midpoint, C, at 48.

Here are two examples of how A, B, and C could be positioned, but there are infinitely many possibilities.

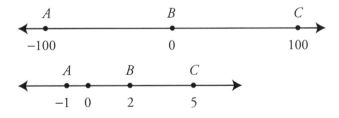

A. If $\overline{AB} > 4$, then half of its distance must be greater than 2. Thus, $\overline{CB} > 2$. This MUST BE TRUE.
B. Point C does not have to be zero. This COULD be true, but doesn't have to be. Do NOT select B.
C. Since C is the midpoint of $\overline{AB}$, this MUST BE TRUE.
D. Since $\overline{AB} > 4$, one-half of its length, or $\overline{AC}$, cannot be equal to 2. This is definitely FALSE.
E. This COULD be but does not have to be true (see the second example above). Do NOT select F.
F. $\overline{AB}$ is twice $\overline{AC}$ since C is the midpoint of $\overline{AB}$. This MUST BE TRUE.
G. This COULD be but does not have to be true (see the first example above). Do NOT select G.

A quick speed note: since you know only three of the choices can be true, if you're sure about your three answers, you can ignore the others. For instance, you might have been able to disregard G completely if you'd already selected A, C, and F. Another way to proceed quickly is to note that, because so little about this number line is fixed, the one thing we're really sure about is that the midpoint is, by definition, in the middle. That would allow you to pick out C and F right away. Then you're only searching for one more correct answer.

The correct answer is A, C, and F.

4. **6:** If you have memorized your Pythagorean triples (or "special right triangles"), the 3–4–5 triangle might have leapt to mind.

If not, try combinations of consecutive integers until you get a valid right triangle. (Use the Pythagorean Theorem to see if you have a valid right triangle. The Third Side Rule would also eliminate some possibilities).

Since the perimeter is less than 15, we know to start small:

1–2–3	$1^2 + 2^2 \neq 3^2$	NOT A RIGHT TRIANGLE
2–3–4	$2^2 + 3^2 \neq 4^2$	NOT A RIGHT TRIANGLE
3–4–5	$3^2 + 4^2 = 5^2$	RIGHT TRIANGLE!

A 3–4–5 triangle must have the longest side, 5, as its hypotenuse. Thus, the legs are 3 and 4. From $A = \frac{1}{2}bh$, $A = \frac{1}{2}(3)(4) = 6$.

The answer is 6.